The Death and Life of State Repression

T0355220

The Death and Life of State Repression

Understanding Onset, Escalation, Termination, and Recurrence

CHRISTIAN DAVENPORT
BENJAMIN J. APPEL

OXFORD
UNIVERSITY PRESS

OXFORD
UNIVERSITY PRESS

Oxford University Press is a department of the University of Oxford.
It furthers the University's objective of excellence in research, scholarship,
and education by publishing worldwide. Oxford is a registered trade mark of
Oxford University Press in the UK and certain other countries.

Published in the United States of America by Oxford University Press
198 Madison Avenue, New York, NY 10016, United States of America.

Cataloging-in-Publication data is on file at Library of Congress

ISBN 978-0-19-765492-7 (pbk.)
ISBN 978-0-19-765537-5 (hbk.)

DOI: 10.1093/oso/9780197654927.001.0001
DOI: 10.1093/oso/9780197655375.001.0001

1 3 5 7 9 8 6 4 2

Printed in Canada

For Eivind and Noah so that they may create as well as live in a better world

Preface

Most individuals that rigorously study state repression/human rights violations do so because they wish to end it. This work lacks the emotion and passion of writing emerging from victims, activists, advocates, and artists as it is intended for a different audience: academics, policymakers, and advocates. Nevertheless, this work is generally guided by the same objectives. Although the underlying motivation of the research is straightforward (especially when you speak with the individuals creating it), there has been little systematic attention given to the topic of ending large-scale, severe (violent) repression (hereafter LSSR). When challenged to think about what was worth doing in 2010 (when we initiated the research discussed in this book), we began on our journey to shed as much light on this topic as possible.

Admittedly, our first exploration was something of a failure as it was too much influenced by conventional thinking which prevails to this day (provided in the Appendix). Accordingly, we laid out the standard theoretical argument underlying almost all work on state repression and we zeroed in on the part of the theory that most believed to be relevant for reducing government repressive behavior—"costs" (i.e., those things that were believed to negatively impact political leaders for engaging in LSSRs like salaries and lost reputation). For this study, we operationalized LSSR with the Political Instability Task Force's database on 41 genocides (ethnically targeted mass killing) and politicides (politically targeted mass killing) from 1955 to 2005 and we operationalized costs by looking at economic sanctions and military interventions, perhaps two of the most prominent solutions put forward in the literature as well as diverse policy circles to this day. From this research, we found support for the role played by costs. Economic sanctions reduced LSSR spells after about three to five years following their implementation and impartial military interventions decreased LSSR spells after about two years following their implementation.

While useful for beginning our thinking about LSSR, there were several limitations with this study that prompted us to rethink and deepen our investigation—leading to the current book.

First, it was unclear how the Political Instability Task Force (PITF) collected their data and what genocides/politicides were. The measure only highlighted a small set of the relevant cases we were interested in (i.e., LSSRs categorized as genocide and politicide). These designations were made without clear coding rules and with no discussion of cases that came close but that did not quite meet whatever criteria were employed by PITF. This led us to search for a better dependent variable.

Second, after reading more extensively, we began to rethink the standard theoretic model that was used to frame research on repression. A large part of this involved identifying puzzles that studies were seemingly incapable of addressing: e.g., accounting for the consistent statistical as well as substantive importance of lagged repression and explaining why domestic factors (i.e., those involving actors and dynamics taking place inside nation-governments) consistently seemed more important than over international ones (i.e., those involving actors and dynamics taking place outside nation-governments). This led us to search for a better theory.

Third, we began to realize that termination was only one part of what one could think of as a repressive "life cycle"—the beginning, application, and end of a sustained level of repressive action. This led us to conclude that for us to truly understand what influenced LSSR we had to more fully embrace "spells" as a unit of analysis and accordingly shift theorization, data collection, and analysis.

Set on our path, we began a series of reconceptualizations and investigations that led to the current manuscript. Now, one would imagine that it is an exceptionally good time to produce a book such as this within a political environment that seems very receptive to human rights in many ways. Indeed, the Biden administration has promised a commitment to human rights and finding out a way to improve them. But the topic of interest has been there for quite some time. For example, President Barack Obama once said that:

66 years since the Holocaust and 17 years after Rwanda, the United governments still lacks a comprehensive policy framework and a corresponding interagency mechanism for preventing and responding to mass atrocities and genocide.   *US President Barack Obama, 2013*

Even President Donald Trump signed into law that:

It shall be the policy of the United States to . . . identify, prevent, and respond to the causes of atrocities, including insecurity, mass displacement, violent conflict, and other conditions that may lead to such atrocities.

Elie Wiesel Genocide and Atrocities Prevention Act of 2018

President Biden extends this concern to yet another administration. At a dedication to a human rights center in Connecticut, he says quite frankly that:

Nuremberg forced us to look closely at the evil of humankind and what we're capable of perpetrating, to see mass atrocities, crimes against humanity do not happen by accident. They don't happen by accident. They are the result of choices—choices made by individual human beings and world leaders.

And sadly, when we look around the world today, we cannot say that the specter of atrocity is behind us.

We see today the patterns, the choices playing out around the world even as we speak: the oppression and use of forced labor of the Uyghurs in Xinjiang; the treatment of the Rohingya by the military junta in Burma; the rampant abuses, including the use of starvation and sexual violence, to terrorize civilian populations in Northern Ethiopia.

Whenever we hear that kind of poisonous hatred, wherever we see our fellow humans being dehumanized, it doesn't mean we go to war, but we must speak out. Silence—as my dad would remind me—silence is complicity. Silence is complicity. That's what Nuremberg said: Your silence is complicity.   *US President Joseph Biden 2021*

Despite the consistent interest, however, the question of what might have a negative impact on large-scale, severe repression has not been addressed. With this in mind, we hope that our efforts provide some assistance as we collectively struggle to figure out what can/should be done in order as well as what cannot/should not be done to prevent, reduce, and stop state-sponsored violent behavior around the globe—perhaps one of the worst phenomenon to befall humanity since the founding of the modern nation-state.

Christian Davenport and Benjamin J. Appel

Acknowledgments

In many respects, this book represents dueling influences. On the one hand, there were a large number of people that provided useful criticisms, insightful suggestions, and positive motivation who deserve to be mentioned. This includes first and foremost Ragnhild Nordås (who sat through almost all versions of this project offering her critical and careful comments along the way as well as the ever-important pause), the Russell Sage Foundation and numerous fellows that were there that year who assisted me in understanding what was worth doing—something we don't do enough, I also wish to thank members of the Conflict and Peace Research and Development Group (CPRD) at the University of Michigan, several individuals at the Peace Research Institute Oslo (especially the great Scott Gates and Håvard Nygård), attendees at the The International Relations Faculty Colloquium at Princeton University, attendees of a presentation at the Arizona State University political science department (including the late/great Will Moore who provided useful comments—as he always did), attendees of a presentation at the political science department of Colombia University and attendees at a panel at the Annual Meeting of the International Studies Association. On the other hand, there were a few people that provided unhelpful criticism, non-insightful suggestions and generally negative vibes who also deserve to be mentioned. This includes basically one individual in every audience where this work was presented, including one very special fellow at the Russell Sage Foundation the year I was there. Finally, I wish to thank my co-author and dear, dear friend Benjamin Appel for joining me on this journey. Ben is that type of person that you want with you on a book or article or desert island for he maintains that wonderful balance of an even temper, an ever-exploratory mind, incredible rigor, creativity, and a peaceful resolution to follow the truth wherever it may lead.

Christian Davenport

I was single and in graduate school at the University of Maryland when Christian and I started working together on a paper that eventually became the basis for this book. I am now married with a son and an associate professor at the University of California, San Diego. It's been a long process, and I owe a debt of gratitude to the many friends, colleagues, and mentors that have helped me along the way. First and foremost, I am grateful to my friend and co-author, Christian. It was a privilege and an honor to write this book with him. Christian is a brilliant scholar with a deep passion for understanding state repression. This is not just an academic pursuit for him, but rather a personal commitment to advancing human rights in the world today. To be sure, his passion and determination, which is so admirable, kept me motivated to finish the book. I also learned so much from him during this project. He is exceptional at crafting and presenting arguments and asking and answering the important academic and policy questions. Simply put, I am so grateful that Christian is my co-author on this, my first book. I also owe a special thank you to my advisors and friends from graduate school, Paul Huth and Sarah Croco. Paul's guidance helped me to become the scholar that I am today, and Sarah was not only essential in helping me academically, but she was also my life coach during graduate school. I wouldn't have made it without her support. I am grateful for my friendship with Alyssa Prorok, who helped me to survive graduate school and the tenure-track. I wrote most of the book during my time at Michigan State University. MSU is a special place full of amazing and supportive people and scholars. I owe a special thank you to both Mike Colaresi and Chuck Ostrom. Mike always challenged me to conduct better research including my work on this book and Chuck helped to transform the department into a special place and always supported me personally and professionally. I finished the book during my first year at the University of California, San Diego. I am grateful to Emilie Hafner-Burton and Pete Cowhey who were instrumental in getting me a job here. Finally, my family. My wonderful and amazing parents really made this all possible with their unconditional love and support. I owe them so much which I will never be able to repay. My mom also loves to ask me the tough questions about my research including my work on this book. My research is certainly better because of it, and I appreciate her interest and thoughtfulness. To my dear son, Noah, who I love and adore so much. Writing a book and struggling with the writing process is so much easier when I know that I have his happy, loving, and smiling face to come home to every night. And last by certainly not least, I thank my brilliant and beautiful wife, Jakana. She has been by my side for most of this book, supporting me through the difficult times and celebrating the happy ones. I couldn't have written this book without her love and support. I am forever grateful for her.

BJA

Contents

List of Figures

List of Tables

Count up the results of fifty years of human rights mechanisms, thirty years of multibillion dollar development programmes and endless high-level rhetoric and the general impact is quite underwhelming...this is a failure of implementation on a scale that shames us all.

Mary Robinson, United Nations Human Rights Commissioner,
1998

(T)here is a growing acceptance that while sovereign states have the primary responsibility to protect their own citizens from (violent) catastrophes, when they are unable or unwilling to do so that responsibility should be taken up by the wider international community— with it spanning a continuum involving prevention, response to violence, if necessary, and rebuilding shattered societies.

Kofi Annan, United Nations Secretary-General, 2003

Introduction

Large-scale, severe repression[1] enacted by political authorities (hereafter LSSR) has been raging in Sudan,[2] off and on for approximately four decades.[3] During this important time, contrary to arguments put forth by some individuals (Power 2013), neither the United States in particular nor the world in general sat idly by when state-sponsored violence was occurring. Rather, almost throughout the whole period that the Sudanese government was engaging in arrests, torture, disappearance, and mass killing between 1976 and 2006 (the time of interest to the current book), diverse institutions (from around the world) discussed and implemented a number of policies in order to stop the violence. The activities put forward have not been particularly unique to Sudan. Indeed, they fit within the standard set of solutions generally put forward for ending government repressive action. These are advanced by politicians, activists, advocates, victims, and scholars from every corner of the globe but they are commonly associated with the United States and the West. The list of solutions/policies is very telling for it reveals a great deal about how most conceive of and (we will argue) misperceive the problem of LSSR.

For example, there have been those that sought to raise awareness of the Sudanese situation, naming/shaming political leaders directly involved in large-scale severe repression (i.e., President Omal El Bashir, Vice President Ali Osman Taha, and National Security Chief Salah Abdala Gosh).

---

[1] Government repression refers to diverse coercive and forceful activities that are used by governments against those within their territorial jurisdiction for the purposes of constraining, harming, or eliminating the targets, their behavior, and/or thoughts (Goldstein 1978; Tilly 1978b; Davenport 2007). This generally involves physical activities directed toward the injury, constraint, and destruction of the human body and/or mind. As conceived, repression encompasses a wide variety of activities: genocide/politicide, massacres, torture, disappearances, beatings, mass arrest, intimidation, as well as covert action (physical and electronic surveillance and the use of informants/agents provocateur). These would fit under diverse categories: (1) violations of First Amendment–type rights, (2) due process in the enforcement and adjudication of law, and (3) personal integrity or security.

[2] Most became aware of this violence after it was designated as a genocide but many were familiar with state-sponsored behavior before this time.

[3] While this problem applies up to the present day, we will principally discuss the 30-year period between 1976 and 2006 to be consistent with the investigation evaluated throughout the manuscript.

The Death and Life of State Repression: Understanding Onset, Escalation, Termination, and Recurrence.
Christian Davenport and Benjamin J. Appel, Oxford University Press. © Oxford University Press 2022.
DOI: 10.1093/oso/9780197655375.003.0001

Such awareness was intended to compel the actors to stop their use of violence so as not to damage their international/domestic legitimacy or to sway individuals/groups not directly involved in the relevant political conflict-inducing them to take some form of action against the offending actors. The mechanisms of awareness and targeted leaders varied.

Some, like Human Rights Watch (HRW), publicly and regularly put out calls to action, informative press releases, and reports, as well as commentary in diverse venues: i.e., the *New York Sun*, the *Los Angeles Times*, the *Wall Street Journal*, the *International Herald Tribune*, the *Globe*, and *Mail*, among others.[4] These were not the only information efforts. Using a webpage, hiring a PR firm, and sending a camera crew to Darfur to film what was taking place as well as supporting "rolling protests" throughout the world (in front of Sudanese embassies and advising other human rights campaigns), Darfur Genocide provided detailed information about what was transpiring and they prompted concerned individuals/organizations to contact the US President at the time (George W. Bush) to demand that the United States government "end the genocide." Some took the effort to host the Olympics as an opportunity to shame the Chinese government into not supporting genocide. A connected effort led Steven Spielberg to step away from his involvement with the opening ceremony. Utilizing an interactive simulation of life as a Sudanese displaced person, Camp Darfur attempted to sensitize individuals to the horrors of government violence in Sudan. The Camp also served as a sign of visible, collective protest when individuals convened like during the campus protests of the anti-apartheid era. The US Holocaust Museum's Committee of Conscience and Stop Genocide Now provided information about who did what to whom as they pushed concerned individuals to contact the media (demanding more attention for the subject) as well as their government representatives (for action) and in an effort to get involved with local community efforts. Related to this, Darfur Scores posted information about the voting records of US Congressional members regarding their (in)action on diverse bills relevant to the topic: e.g., Darfur Accountability Act (S495), Darfur Peace and Accountability Act (S1462), and Resolution on Civilian Protection (S393). Numerous films have also been developed to assist with raising awareness including *Darfur Diaries* (2006), *Darfur Now*

---

[4] HRW not only provided information about what was taking place but also suggested specific policies that would exclude the Darfur leaders held responsible from "interactions of a ceremonial nature...including courtesy calls, receptions, photo opportunities, attendance at national day celebrations and so on." In an older period, this would be referred to as "shunning."

(2007), *On Our Watch* (2007), *Sand and Sorrow* (2007), and *The Devil Came on Horseback* (2007).

Not believing that attention alone would produce an effect, others pursued what was believed to be a more direct and impactful approach. Here, some advocated threatening and implementing the use of economic sanctions against Sudanese political authorities. These activities were suggested because it was believed that LSSRs would end when outsiders threatened the economic livelihood of the offending regime. For example, there were numerous efforts undertaken by US political leaders with this approach in mind.[5] Drawing on the International Emergency Economic Powers Act, the National Emergencies Act, and the United States government's code, on November 11th, 1997, President Bill Clinton issued an Executive Order (#13067) blocking imports, exports, and ending the granting of loans and credits with and to Sudan. Not removed until 2017, this effort was estimated to halt trading between the United States and Sudan that accounted for an estimated 70 million dollars annually. Similarly, Governor Rick Perry signed a bill divesting the Employees Retirement System of Texas as well as the government Teacher Retirement System of Texas from companies that supported Sudan because of its genocidal behavior. Seventeen states within the United States adopted comparable divestment policies.

The approach of economic sanctions was not only limited to US politicians and state governments. Diverse NGOs and INGOs adopted a similar approach. For example, in order to sanction those involved with Sudanese LSSR, the Sudan Divestment Task Force (SDTF) tried to pressure industries to remove their holdings in the region.[6] Unfortunately, the reach of this effort was limited because it could not fully harness the power of an international divestment campaign that would have included Asian interests and investment in Sudanese oil. To address this limitation, in 2009, the SDTF turned into the Conflict Risk Network (CRN) which worked more broadly around the world to influence the Sudanese LSSR through its more extensive economic leverage. Related to this effort, Divest Sudan targeted European and Asian multinationals that provided "critical" economic, commercial, and financial support to relevant political leaders. As stated in promotional material for this initiative: "These companies either support brutally

---

[5] It should be noted that this was not always of their own accord. Often protest and/or petitions were the initial reasons for political leaders paying attention and/or taking action.

[6] Reflecting important overlap in efforts across actors, 10 state governments in the United States followed the SDTF model by targeting Sudanese investment.

destructive oil development and production in southern Sudan, or provide investments that benefit only Khartoum and the surrounding region of northern Sudan." As they continued, "Oil revenues, extracted with the blood of southern Sudanese... sustain a regime that could not survive without this economic lifeline." Similarly, Divest Sudan sought to coordinate all efforts which targeted the "most egregiously (offensive) companies in Sudan" (i.e., those that had a business relationship with the government, imparted minimal benefit to the country, and had no official position regarding the government-sponsored violence in the country).[7] Some even creatively targeted economic supporters of Sudan like China through open criticism of investors like Warren Buffett who maintained considerable amounts of stock in Petro China.

A third group advocated a more militaristic solution. Here, it was believed that LSSRs would end when outsiders sent troops to physically impede the activities of the Sudanese government.[8] For example, some suggested sending in troops like the UNAMID mission (called "United Nations-African Union Hybrid Operation in Darfur"). This effort was comprised of UN Peacekeepers and African Union forces, representing an unprecedented combination of armed groups.[9] Relatedly, Africa Action suggested that the African Union troops in Sudan be "re-hatted" to represent the United

---

[7] Not all followed this idea of applying economic sticks. Drawing on the same laws as President Clinton, on October 17, 2006, President George W. Bush signed an Executive Order (#13412) blocking transactions and blocking engagement with the oil sector between the United States and Sudan. These sanctions, too, were lifted more than a decade after their origin in 2017. "The change (from sticks to carrots) reflect(ed) a strategy shift in how to bring about reforms in Sudan.... Instead of relying solely on punishment via sanctions, the new strategy (was) to use relief to encourage more changes" (Morello 2017).

[8] Others advocate a different but related approach. For example, there is the Safe Demilitarized Border Zone (SDBZ). The creation of the SDBZ in Sudan was agreed to on September 27, 2012, between the governments of Sudan and South Sudan. Beyond the scope of the current study, it is still worthwhile to quickly discuss it. The tension informing the decision involved the political disputes between the two nations, only indirectly was this influenced by the genocidal actions and support for rebel groups on either side of the border. The commitment to the SDBZ never came to fruition in 2012. It was reasserted however in 2013. Leaders from both governments re-agreed to mark the undisputed part of their almost 2,000 km (1,200 miles) long border. The region was supposed to be monitored by the UN peacekeeping force in Abyei (UNISFA) as part of the Joint Border Verification Monitoring Mechanism (JBVMM). Many on both sides feared this buffer zone, with the removal of troops, it was believed that this would entail the removal of safety. The Satellite Sentinel Project revealed (in May 2013) that Sudan and South Sudan failed to meet their full obligations to withdraw their troops in two potential hot spots along their shared border, these being Heglig and Kiir Adem. In 2018, Sudan and South Sudan leaders activated (rather, reactivated) the demilitarized zone. The agreement leading to this implementation is not publicly available, but according to the Sudan Tribune, their decision after meeting "activate[s] the joint cooperation agreement signed in 2012, renewing commitment to work together to achieve security and stability in both countries."

[9] Between 2007 and 2017, this group increased in number after which the forces began to decrease.

Nations and that 20,000 additional UN troops needed to be deployed in order to potentially deter violent behavior and enforce the peace agreement. Other efforts went further than just suggesting that troops be sent in and provided ideas as to what specifically the troops should do when they were deployed. For example, Amnesty International urged the African Union to send in troops comprised of African Union as well as the UN members in an effort to disarm the relevant repressive agents (most notably the Janjaweed).

A fourth group advocated imposing legal sanctions. In this context, it was believed that LSSRs would stop when diverse laws and responsibilities were invoked as laid out by different international laws. Here, the fear regarding the loss of reputation and/or additional punishments was expected to compel those responsible for large-scale repression to withdraw from the offending activity. For example, at one point, the International Criminal Court (ICC) issued warrants for two individuals who were accused of committing 51 acts of war crimes, including murder, rape, torture, forcible displacement, and persecution to work. This action required that the Sudanese government turn over the relevant perpetrators pursuant to their obligations under Security Council Resolution (SCR) 1593. Further invoking 1593, the group Justice for Darfur encouraged the Security Council to adopt a resolution that called on the government of Sudan to cooperate with its earlier ruling, stating that the Security Council needed to follow up until war criminals were brought before the ICC.

A fifth group combined the different approaches identified above. For example, in September of 2004, Human Rights Watch released a statement "What You Can Do about Darfur" which listed numerous approaches including naming and shaming/spreading awareness (i.e., informing oneself, writing to local newspapers, holding a video screening, writing to the members of the United Nations Security Council to condemn the Sudanese government) as well as taking military action, specifically suggesting the deployment of UNAMID forces for the maintenance of peace in the region. The Genocide Intervention Network advocated imposing sanctions on oil, arms, assets, and travel for those involved in the LSSR as well as creating a no-fly zone and supporting African Union intervention. Similarly, Save Darfur advanced a detailed multi-prong approach. First, they engaged in raising awareness. They asked congress for a national weekend of prayer and reflection on Darfur. They started a website and a postcard campaign called "A Million Voices for Darfur" which was intended to flood the US President with notes about the crisis. Save Darfur sponsored a media event intended to raise awareness, with ads in subways in NYC, in national newspapers, and on TV and magazines, featuring famous celebrities (observed by one of the authors of this book numerous times while in residence). They also pushed activists across the country to contact senators on the Armed Forces Committee and request military action. A different organization, Human Rights First (HRF) suggested that media attention needed to be shed on the Sudanese problem, the UN should be pressured to send troops, and that sanctions should be imposed against the government (if the Sudanese government didn't suspend violent activities).

Other approaches were less extensive but revealed a similar hybridic approach. For example, The International Crisis Group (ICG) released a highly visible videogame "Darfur is Dying" in order to raise awareness. In addition to freezing assets, they also advocated that Sudanese offshore accounts be investigated and that Chadian forces be deployed to the border in an effort to threaten the Sudanese government. Students Taking Action Now: Darfur (STAND) called for young people to educate others about what was taking place, push public officials to take some kind of action, and to prompt colleges, companies, and governments to divest from Sudan. Finally, the Darfur Rehabilitation Project advocated deploying UN troops and disarming the Janjaweed and prosecuting guilty government officials in the newly created International Criminal Court.

Interestingly, the list of activities above focused on organizations and activities that originated outside of Sudan, reflecting something of an "international" approach. There have been others however that maintained that the LSSR in Sudan could only be resolved by the Sudanese themselves—reflecting something of a "domestic" approach. For example, some have called for civil disobedience and mass resistance within the country in order to stop the government-sponsored violence. Some protests and acts of civil disobedience began when the LSSR started but most of the noteworthy demonstrations came in later years during the time of the Arab Spring which extends beyond our time period of interest but does merit a quick mention. Addressing this aspect of the case is useful because although LSSR in Sudan has frequently been an important component of the anti-regime sentiment, it was only one of the many grievances that were raised. Following successes in Tunisia and Egypt, thousands of young Sudanese took to the streets in protest, against the government, its wounded economy, rising prices, and political repression. Later in that year, Darfuri student activists called for a revolution and declared their open support for the Sudan Revolutionary

Front fighting the government in the south, protesting also the displacement of Manasir peoples. Interestingly, once civil conflict emerged, the repressive response of the government to these activities was added to the list of demands made by those challenging the regime. During these activities, security forces killed dozens and crackdowns became commonplace among those expressing opposition views. Additionally, the government used bombs to crush diverse civil resistance efforts as well as to target rebel groups. Here, it was believed that mass mobilization would be able to hinder/stop repression either by signaling the significant dissatisfaction of the citizenry or by removing the offending actors from office.

By any stretch of the imagination, the sheer breadth and variety of solutions/policies put forward to deal with LSSR in Sudan was impressive.[10] Invariably, however, one is led to ask a very simple question: did anything work? Did the sanctions, threats, mobilization, film, and other activities have any impact whatsoever on large-scale repressive behavior in Sudan between 1976 and 2006? According to the Political Terror Scale data on human rights violations (discussed in more detail later), the answer appears to be no: the government of Sudan was at or above a three on the scale for the entire period across the majority of sources consulted, which is a code that would be applied if state repression was large-scale and severe. Why is this? Why did nothing appear to work? Below, we will argue that this is because none of the efforts employed significantly perturbed the cohort of individuals who came together to develop as well as implement the repressive policy of interest.

The first piece of evidence for this conclusion concerns the fact that since independence in 1956 the Sudanese military has maintained an important influence (if not stranglehold) over politics in general and state-sponsored use of violence in particular. With coups in the 1950s, 1969, 1971, and 1989 as well as an unsuccessful attempt in 1976 (precisely when our study begins), this position has been reinforced repeatedly. This of course does not mean that the military is alone in its interest in or use of repression. There is a strong historical pattern of subcontracting and utilizing militias to assist state actors in carrying out designated policies. The interest of diverse coercive/forceful

[10] Despite the range, not all have been satisfied that the best solutions have been identified and acted upon. Indeed, perceiving a limited amount of attention and creativity, in a rare moment of candor Nicholas Kristof (*New York Times* editorial writer), asked for additional suggestions about what could/should be done about ending the government violence in Darfur. The sentiment in the editorial was more than appropriate. Indeed, it captured a certain degree of desperation observable throughout the world. Many have looked at the government violence there and wondered what, if anything, could be done to stop it.

wielding actors was further reinforced by the presence of domestic unrest. For example, the first Sudanese civil war took place from 1955 to 1972 and the second between 1983 and 2005.

While the structure of the cohort behind the repressive implementation in Sudan was not uniformly cohesive, it is clear that under the guidance of Bashir it developed a significant amount of coordination and centralization. For example, there was the creation of the Revolutionary Command Council which served as something of an umbrella organization under which coercive-force wielding institutions were brought together. Also during this time, Bashir appointed himself head of state, prime minister, head of the armed forces, as well as minister of defence. Such a concentration of power around a single individual and cohort was so obvious that some referred to Bashir as "the Spider" at the center of the military-security web. This central and influential cohort became important because we would maintain that without perturbing this group in some fundamental way, repression was and is likely to continue. This becomes crucial to identify because even after Bashir is officially removed from office in 2019 his involvement across other domains is still maintained and repressive behavior largely stays at the level of the LSSR discussed above.

Of course, we need not limit ourselves to the singular case of Sudan. In the face of large-scale, severe repression in China, the former Soviet Union, Cambodia, Chile, Guatemala, South Africa, Kosovo, Rwanda, Syria, and throughout the rest of the world over the last 50 years, the same solutions and policies as those identified above have been put forward by governments, NGOs, INGOs, journalists, celebrities, and ordinary people alike. In many respects, these are the best strategies that have been developed to deal with the problem of LSSR. The question emerging from all these ideas, discussions, and implementations remains clear and quite pressing however: what, if anything, has worked? Despite the importance of this question, we (researchers, policymakers, NGOs, INGOs, journalists, celebrities, and ordinary people) do not really have an answer.

Part of the explanation for this omission concerns the fact that most of those with the greatest interest in the subject (i.e., victims, citizens, advocates, and most politicians) are led to activism, advocacy, and policy implementation and not investigating impact assessment in detail. The actors identified above generally follow their expertise and do what they have been prepared to do/believe in. A lack of interest in an evaluation makes sense for such groups. No advocates of the different solutions identified above have a real interest in discovering that their preferred method (i.e., the one that they have dedicated their lives to, mobilized around, sought funding for, and fought to implement) is unable to work because the relevant individuals/institutions advocating these options would suffer losses of prestige, resources, legitimacy, and meaning. No one suggesting naming/shaming, economic sanctions, or electoral democratization wants to know that their particular solution for ending state repression has no or limited impact on the phenomenon of interest because this information would signal the end of their organization and perhaps their identity. Related, many of those disconnected from the direct implementation of these efforts also have no interest in discovering that different policies do not work because (at the point of discovering the lack of an influence) they would be at a loss regarding what could/should be done when the next crisis was identified.

The academic community is similarly limited in its insights but for somewhat different reasons. For instance, most empirically rigorous social science research has been dedicated to investigating the behavior undertaken by those who challenge political authorities (i.e., protesters in protest, terrorists in terrorism, insurgents in civil war, and revolutionaries in revolution). Comparatively less effort has been directed toward evaluating the violence undertaken by governments. Even those that do study state repression and human rights violations however have been unable to shed much light on what ends this behavior because they have been mostly focused on understanding "variation"—i.e., how a particular independent variable increases or decreases government coercive and forceful behavior (Poe and Neal Tate 1994; Poe, Tate, and Keith 1999; Davenport 1995; Davenport and Armstrong 2004; Nordås and Davenport 2013; Simmons 2009; Hafner-Burton 2005; Hafner-Burton 2008; Kathman and Wood 2011; Keith, Tate, and Poe 2009a; Ritter and Conrad 2016; Krain 1997a, 2005; Hill and Jones 2014; Davenport 2007; Møller and Skaaning 2013; Zanger 2000; Appel 2018).

While useful for getting a general impression of what influences state-sponsored repressive action, this approach is limited because it treats all values of and movements in repression as though they were equally interesting (e.g., movements from a 2 to a 1 on the Political Terror Scale are deemed to be the same as movements from a 3 to a 2—discussed in greater detail below). This is not how most outside of the academy think about the topic however. While some government repression is accepted (the price paid for establishing and maintaining domestic order/being out of the socio-political hell described by Hobbes), what is not really tolerated, deemed acceptable, and/or legitimate involves large-scale violent government activity directed against those within the relevant territorial jurisdiction. Such is the predominant focus of those interested in human rights violation, atrocities, genocide, politicide, one-sided violence, government terror, and government repression. There is a fundamental difference however between variation in repression on the one hand and preventing, decreasing, hindering, and entirely stopping the possible recurrence of large-scale, severe repression on the other. Indeed, these two involve very different conceptions, different theories, data, and methods of analysis.

In addition to this, insights are limited in academic research because empirically oriented scholars tend to be especially interested in particular independent variables; for example Simmons (2009) is fundamentally interested in international law while Keck and Sikkink (2014) are fundamentally interested in human rights organizations. Although useful in focusing discussion, zooming in like this is not useful for evaluating the most comprehensive models and/or using the most valid measures for variables included within relevant analyses.[11]

Clearly, it is not the case that all researchers have ignored the topic of ending state repression. Highlighting one or a few solutions, some have focused on the onset and termination of government repression that is less severe than an LSSR (Ritter 2014). A version of the question regarding termination has been explored by research specifically interested in stopping torture (Conrad and Moore 2010) as well as by research specifically interested in stopping genocide (Bellamy 2015). The first piece highlights a few of the explanatory factors/policies identified above and examines them in a rigorous manner but only with regard to a specific form of state repression that is less severe, more individualistic in its approach, and generally less violent. The second piece highlights a greater number of factors identified above but (again) only with regard to a particular form of state repression. Beyond these studies there has been no systematic effort undertaken toward evaluating a broader set of policies as well as broader conceptualization of large-scale state-sponsored behavior. This omission is not a common feature with other forms of large-scale political conflict and violence. Indeed,

[11] For example, both Hafner-Burton as well as Simmons include a problematic conception of democracy within their analyses which include components of civil conflict in its measurement and they investigate the relationship in a linear manner despite revelations that the impact is non-linear as well as interactive with behavioral challenges.

over time, there has developed an extensive literature on understanding and explaining how interstate and civil wars begin, vary, end, and recur.[12]

More directly on topic, but still largely unhelpful for the purposes of understanding general patterns, are more historical, qualitative inquiries (e.g., Power (2013)). Here, we find detailed discussion regarding many of the same solutions/policies identified above to stop repression. Unfortunately, the conclusions drawn from this work are limited for several reasons: (1) these researchers have not consistently defined, identified, and operationalized relevant government behavior—gauging increases and decreases effectively; and (2) these studies have not considered alternative explanations as the researchers tend to focus on singular international or domestic explanations—avoiding the topic of controls and confounding factors altogether.

This omission is unfortunate because it is commonly understood that, in the context of violent behavior, the greatest amount of damage done to human kind has been done by (their own) governments. By some estimates, political authorities have killed and/or injured more individuals than all the victims of interstate and civil war as well as non-state terrorism combined (e.g., Rummel (2002)).[13] With these observations in mind, we concluded that it was time that our understanding of LSSR should at least be raised to the level of other forms of political conflict and violence—if not beyond them. When one carefully considers the subject, however, the complexity of the topic, the necessity for additional investigation as well as the restructuring of analyses become readily apparent. We discuss the various changes that must take place below.

0.1 Spells

To begin the type of analysis suggested above, it needs to first be clearly understood that ending government repression involves addressing and understanding a larger process—a repressive spell or "life" cycle with a beginning (i.e., the onset of the specific spell), middle (i.e., where applications are underway that could escalate or de-escalate), end (i.e., termination of the

---

[12] Endings have also been explored in the area of terrorism and nonviolent direct action.

[13] If one adds in activities such as violent policing as well as government-sponsored criminal justice activities like mass incarceration and execution, this likely goes even higher—these are beyond the scope of the current research however.

spell), and potential recurrence (i.e., where a new spell begins involving the same political authorities). This is not to say that all parts of this process are equally interesting to all individuals—indeed, we began this project most interested with stopping ongoing LSSRs in part because we were skeptical about the commitment to prevent these from occurring before they were underway or preventing them recurring. Rather, this is to say that in order to understand government repression and what influences it, it is necessary to identify and examine the different phases of repressive spells at the same time. It is an empirical question whether the determinants of onset, degrees of violence during the spell, termination, and recurrence are driven by the same factors. To date, this insight has been lost on/ignored by researchers focusing on repressive behavior and human rights violation because the different aspects of a spell have never been systematically evaluated. To our knowledge, there have been many investigations of variation, a few investigations of onset, but no evaluations of escalation, termination, and/or recurrence.

Does it make sense to import the idea of "spells" from other forms of political conflict and violence into the area of human rights/government repression—especially when much of this work suggests that many interventions do not reduce or, worse yet, make conflicts more violent as well as longer (e.g., Regan and Aydin (2006))? We believe that the answer is yes. Researchers, policymakers, activists, victims, perpetrators, journalists, and ordinary citizens conceive of, write about, and discuss large-scale repressive behavior by explicitly employing the language of spells without ever calling them this. What were the Stalinist purges, the terror of the Pol Pot era, the violence in Rwanda during 1994, or the genocide in Darfur but sustained large-scale, violent, government spells with resources, actors, and actions being repeatedly mobilized over time and space? Individuals that investigated and attempted to halt these activities were not concerned with discrete, isolated events—although many were deemed particularly offensive and/or illegal. Instead, individuals were interested with understanding a series of linked activities that they deemed to be unacceptable. At first the concern is with onset but after the initiation of a spell, the overriding concern became finding some intervention (some policy) that would bring the relevant behavior (i.e., the spell) to an end as well as preventing the relevant behavior from occuring again. Finally, while there are some variables in the relevant literature that consistently receive support (e.g., democracy, economic development, and population), there is a large number of variables which comprise the go-to solutions for addressing state repression (e.g., economic sanctions, military intervention, naming/shaming, and signing/ratifying human rights treaties) that have received mixed support. One explanation for this varied impact might be that the different policies only apply to specific phases of the repressive life cycle or they only matter indirectly through some other variable. Again, this has never been examined explicitly and thus we do not know, but it is something worth investigating because the answers would be extremely important.

Conceptually, the life-cycle approach being discussed here generally is in line with the extensive historical literature on government repression within individual countries (Goldstein (1978) and Dallin, Breslauer, et al. (1970))— this literature frequently speaks of spells, campaigns, episodes, programs, missions, and the like. The framing also follows the suggestions of those interested in the call to "Never Again" allow LSSR to ravage the lives of those living within nation-states such as (1) preventing relevant activities from emerging in the first place (i.e., onset and recurrence) and (2) stopping these activities from continuing once they are underway (i.e., escalation and termination).[14]

Such an approach is complex as each component of the life cycle requires conceptualization, measurement, and analysis. Such an approach is crucial though (for researchers, policymakers, advocates, activists, as well as funders) because it reorients and pivots the systematic study of government repression in an important direction. For example, analyzing repressive behavior (the topic of interest) as a spell involves different conceptualization because spells are very different units compared to years, quarters, weeks, and/or days. Analyzing repressive behavior as a spell involves different theorization because it suggests a very different causal process driving the relevant phenomenon. Indeed, we will maintain that LSSR's are influenced by only certain variables within estimated models as a certain degree of momentum comes to be built into the implementation of repression. Here, the key to understanding what would work resides in acknowledging that a central core of individuals and institutions comes to be involved in the repressive policy. Similar to existing research, we believe that these individuals and institutions conceive of the objectives to be pursued, they collect information to be evaluated in the decision regarding what should be done,

---

[14] There was a third element to this as well which was was concerned with prosecuting those engaged in violent state behavior after they had ended. This is not examined within this book, but it is something of a natural extension that should be undertaken.

they make a determination to engage in LSSR, and then they implement relevant behavior. Differing from existing research, however, in what we refer to as the "juggernaut" theory of state repression, we believe that after the decision to use repression has been made and relevant behavior is enacted, the cohort surrounding this decision effectively closes the door to generating new information, updating old information, and entertaining other policy options. In this context, perturbance of the repressive cohort becomes crucial for understanding all aspects of a repressive spell.

With this orientation, our understanding of this process involves identifying shifts in cohort composition and the reasons for them. If (as most suggest) large-scale government violence represents a strategy employed by government officials who are essentially desperate and unable to wield any other mechanism of influence over their populations, then at the critical moment of threat relevant actors would have few concerns other than surviving the crisis that they are subject to. This would render them ill-concerned with what other politicians, NGOs, and citizens say about them or the profitability of economic relations—basically most of the solutions/policies/strategies suggested used to influence them. Such a realization is important because it makes the imposition of costs, suggested by most researchers as the primary way to impact repression in a negative direction, largely irrelevant. Further differentiating our work from existing research, we do not believe that, once created, cohorts go away after (actual) threats dissipate—another core reason offered for state repression. Rather, we believe that even after threats/behavioral challenges go away, the individual interactions as well as institutional relationships stay in place, reinforcing earlier evaluations of the situation—disregarding small and/or meaningless changes in the political, economic, and demographic environment. Such a realization compels us to better understand why LSSRs begin and escalate before they can get out of hand, why they escalate once underway, why/when they end, as well as why/when they recur.

Following from this, analyzing repression as a spell is important because it involves very different ideas about the subject as well as distinct data collection and estimation procedures from what has been historically examined in the literature. As a consequence of this reorientation, all findings in this line of inquiry (derived up to this point) should be viewed as being at risk of not being supported at all or only being significant for certain parts of a spell. In this way we allow for the possibility that there are no simplistic answers to the problem of government repression viewed across its life cycle and all that we feel we know about state repression derived over the last 40 years is under scrutiny.

0.2 Evaluating All Reasonable Solutions

Second, it is clear that an evaluation of policies/variables regarding the end of government repression must be inclusive. Researchers cannot/should not be allowed to focus on only the variables that they find to be most important, ignoring other variables as well as innovations in measurement and established practices that have been discovered in their evaluation. Rather, researchers need to consider the impact of a diverse set of policies/variables on different phases of the repressive process as well as attend to various improvements that have been made in the investigation of government repression.

This approach deviates from the current practice of the literature that tends to be divided along perceived driving forces. For example, to domestic scholars repressive behavior is believed to be influenced by factors that exist within nation-states such as political democracy, political conflict/violence (e.g., civil war and nonviolent direct action), economic development, and issues regarding socio-political order (associated with population size and youth bulges). For international scholars, repressive behavior is believed to be influenced by factors that exist outside of nation-states such as naming/shaming, military intervention, economic sanctions, and the signing/ratification international treaties.

A different hybridic view combines the two approaches. Here, it is possible that both domestic as well as international factors can help address the weaknesses of the other. For example, international actors might not have the local level contacts or the best ideas regarding what could/should be done to assist in mobilizing individuals (held by domestic actors) but they might have a comparative advantage in generating resources and/or providing information to donors as well as outside audiences. Accordingly, there are two views of this. On the one hand, it is possible that repression is largely driven by some factors within nation-states along with some factors outside of those territorial jurisdictions. Here, it is important to be attentive to sequences and timing because at some parts of the repressive life cycle certain policies/variables might be important and within different parts other policies/variables might be important. On the other hand, it is possible that repression is driven by some factors within nation-states because of their connection with factors outside of the relevant territorial jurisdiction. For example, democratic practices are often influenced or paid/pushed for, by agencies outside of the nation in question by providing financial backing and training. Additionally, some outside of nation-states assist protestors within a country to further their efforts. Again, neither of these scenarios has previously been examined across the repressive life cycle.

Now, although we believe that both domestic and international factors could play a role and should be examined, it is not the case that we believe they do. In particular, we believe that domestic factors will have more importance because they are more relevant to how, where and when cohorts are generated/dissolved as well as how, where and why repressive behavior is employed. Moreover, we believe that two variables in particular—the level of electoral democracy and increases in this level (i.e., electoral democratization) will have the greatest importance on spells because of their influence on politicians and security force agents who are central members of repressive cohorts. As configured, our investigation will not only provide new insights into state repression but also provide new insights into what policies can work to reduce/eliminate repressive behavior as well as provide some information about when they might work.

0.3 Redesigning the Study of Large-Scale, Severe Repression

To better understand why governments use repressive behavior against those within their territorial jurisdiction at particularly high levels, our research addresses the various factors identified above.

Within the first chapter, we review the literature, put forward our critique of this work, as well as put forward our juggernaut theory of repression in an effort to address existing limitations. At its core, our argument maintains that repressive behavior is created by and used to protect specific political cohorts—a group of individuals and institutions who come to view government repression as their preferred policy to address a particular need. Viewed in this manner, small changes in relevant explanatory variables are unlikely to shift repressive practices as the nudges contained within them are largely ignored by largely insular and defensive actors. Indeed, what is needed to bring about a change in government behavior is a fundamental disturbance of the cohort that was involved with the institution deciding to begin the spell in the first place.

As designed, our theoretical argument applies to four distinct stages: (1) when the cohort comes into being (onset)—this we maintain is intricately connected with domestic threat perception and the constraint/regulation of centralized government coercion and force through political democracy; (2) when authorities (already within a spell) are prompted to increase the scope and/or degree of violence involved with repressive behavior (i.e., escalation)—this we maintain is connected with an increased sensitivity to a broadened conception of threats within as well as external to the nation-state in question; (3) when the spell ends (i.e., termination)—which we maintain is connected to dismantling the repressive cohort through democratization; and, (4) when an earlier spell (which ended) is renewed (i.e., recurrence)— this we maintain is connected to how far the nation-state has moved from the relevant cohort since the earlier spell.

In the second chapter, we provide a discussion regarding our unit of analysis—the repressive spell, as well as the various dependent variables that emerge from such a conception: onset, escalation, termination and recurrence. Following this, we present the various independent variables that are used to explain why and when state repression occurs. The third through sixth chapters present our analyses of a new dataset regarding the four phases of the life cycle identified above for all 244 LSSR spells from 1976 to 2006. Why this period? Such a question is largely neglected by those who study global as well as country-specific processes but this is useful because the specifics during the analysis are important. During the period in question, the domestic and international communities were interested in the topic and trying a wide variety of policies/practices, there was popular interest in the subject, and around 2001 (following the terrorist attack and global war on terror) it is possible that a different type of relationship exists between democracy and state repression/human rights violation. Reviewing our results, the theoretical argument we advance does quite well, offering important insights into repressive behavior and the policies/solutions that impact it. Each phase and chapter is briefly discussed below.

Examining onset (Chapter 3), we find that domestic factors are more important than international ones in accounting for the beginning of LSSR spells. Here, the negative impact of electoral as well as judicial levels of democracy and electoral movements toward democracy (i.e., democratization) hold the key to prevention. There is one important exception here: international Preferential Trade Agreements (PTAs) which are found to statistically and substantively reduce the likelihood of LSSR onset. This suggests that economic interaction and integration with the global community can reduce the possibility of initiating a large-scale, severe repression. Some hybrid combinations of domestic and international factors are also shown to be important but less stably so: e.g., results disclose that externally supported civil resistance decreases the likelihood of onset but weakly and inconsistently across models.

In line with what existing literature suggests, diverse variables connected with political threats to the regime account for the increased likelihood of onset: e.g., ongoing civil war and population (both domestic factors). This suggests that repressive campaigns are initiated with distinct threats to political authorities in mind. Interestingly, results identify that neutral military interventions (an international factor) increase the likelihood of onset. Here, we find that specific activities undertaken by the international community, presumably to reduce perceptions of threat to government and LSSR, actually have the opposite impact.

In order to better understand our findings, we drill down a little deeper to briefly examine the causes of electoral democratic transitions (our most important independent variable). Examining this topic, we find that externally generated nonviolent campaigns are linked to a greater likelihood of electoral democratic transition. This suggests that domestic-international hybrids are important for preventing the onset of a LSSR revealing both direct and indirect influences. In contrast, generally we find that external factors have little influence on electoral democratization, which lends further support to our primary analysis.

Analyzing escalation (i.e., the increased scope and/or degree of state-sponsored violence), once a spell is underway (Chapter 4), we (once more) find that important influences reside in both the domestic and international environments but (also again) we note that the key to keeping repressive behavior at a lower level of LSSR seems to involve democracy and democratization—both electoral as well as judicial aspects. Differing from the onset of repressive spells which revealed no support for civil resistance, we find that domestically—generated civil resistance plays an important role in reducing the likelihood of escalation. While unable to prevent the beginning of large-scale, severe repression, therefore, mass nonviolent mobilization can prevent these repressive spells from getting worse (once underway). This is interesting in that it reveals that governments are not uniformly threatened by all behavior and thus likely to ramp up repressive behavior. Rather, they can view some challenges as not being worthy of repression.

In line with our theoretical argument that pretexts for expansion of a pre-established policy are important, all other factors examined increase the likelihood of escalation. Regarding domestic factors, this includes ongoing civil war and population. Regarding international factors, this (again) includes pro-government interventions, neutral interventions, as well as economic sanctions.

Acknowledging that we have a different set of cases than is normally discussed in the literature, in an effort to more clearly understand and communicate our most robust policy-oriented variable, we once more examine the causes of democratic transition. Examining this topic, we find that diverse factors matter but fewer than in the investigation of onset. For example, from the domestic environment, we find that civil war and population size tends to increase the likelihood of electoral democratization whereas economic development decreases it. From the international environment, we find that neutral interventions decrease the likelihood of democratization. Finally, results disclose that two domestic-international hybrid variables matter. As found, internationally backed civil resistance movements increase the likelihood of electoral transition as well as strong civil society movements connected to the global community. This (again) reveals indirect influences of the international community on LSSR.

Engaging in an investigation of spell termination (Chapter 5), the topic that we began our research to address, we find that domestic factors are the ones most likely to drive the phenomenon of interest. In line with our argument, we find that electoral democratization and the level of judicial democracy are the only variables that are consistently able to stop large-scale repressive spells once underway and to send them to relatively lower levels of state repression. In contrast, the international factors that are frequently highlighted in the literature, media, and policy circles have no pacifying impact on spell termination at all; indeed, one (human rights NGOs) even prolongs repressive spells!

In line with earlier chapters, to produce insights into the factors that are indirectly associated with the termination of repressive spells, we examine the causes of democratic transition. Analyzing this topic, we find that externally supported nonviolent campaigns are linked to a greater likelihood of democratic transitions. This suggests that the mass campaigns have an important indirect impact on ending LSSR spells. At the same time, we note that in and of themselves these campaigns have no direct impact on spell termination. Indeed, in contrast, external factors are found to have little impact on electoral democratization, which lends further support to our primary analysis.

Finally, examining recurrence (Chapter 6), results disclose that even fewer determinants exist for this phenomenon then the other phases of the repressive life cycle. This said, among those that are identified, the majority are domestic in orientation. For example, electoral democratization is (again) found to have a preventive influence on LSSR resurgence and thus where there is a move to democracy following an LSSR, another spell is less likely to occur. In addition to this, economic development is found to play a pacifying role, whereas population size is found to increase the chances that governments engage in another wave of repressive behavior. The international environment is somewhat mixed in its influence. On the one hand, pro-government interventions tend to decrease the likelihood of LSSR resurgence. On the other hand, neutral interventions tend to increase the likelihood that governments return to high-level repressive practices.

Exploring the determinants of electoral democratization one last time, we find that particular hybrid variables do have an impact. Revealing the importance of specific intersections as well as our theoretical argument, results disclose that internationally backed nonviolent movements and NGO participation increase the likelihood of democratization. Several domestic variables also play a role: e.g., ongoing civil war and past transitions both increase the likelihood of electoral changes in the relevant government. Interestingly, economic development and population tend to decrease the likelihood of electoral democratization. Lastly, comparatively few international variables matter. Here, we find that regional diffusion tends to increase the likelihood of democratization whereas pro-government interventions are negative in their influence.

In Chapter 7, we explore the dynamics identified within the previous four chapters with some case studies. Acknowledging that our investigation is broadly probabilistic, this was done because we decided that it would be useful to discuss particular sequences of institutions and practices where we look at spell onset, democratization, civil resistance, civil war, and spell termination. Specifically, this was done within the cases of South Korea, Chile, Senegal, Albania, Zambia, Poland, Madagascar, Mali, and Thailand.

The book concludes with a call to action as well as a call to reflection. Given the high degree of interest shown by individuals throughout the world with addressing repressive activity, we have outlined numerous things that would need to be done in order to reduce the likelihood, escalation, and recurrence of repression, as well as increase the likelihood of terminating government-sponsored mass repressive behavior. Clearly, the list is not exhaustive but it does provide some concrete suggestions that could be used to guide research as well as policy across a repressive life cycle—something not previously addressed in existing literature. In addition, we also raise several questions which are left remaining for those interested in further advancing beyond the current book. Perhaps the biggest issue identified here is the realization that there are many spells that simply do not end. Some begin and they just continue even in the face of diverse efforts to hinder/stop them. We do not believe that this needs to be the case. Indeed, we suggest that if relevant organizations can act better and more efficiently as a global community (linking domestic and international forces against a more precisely targeted repressive cohort), then they will have a much better chance at disturbing spells and bringing them to an end. A lack of coordination however will leave spells unperturbed and LSSR will continue to wreak havoc on humankind.

1

Old and New Directions in the Study

of State Repression

1.1 Where We Have Been

Beginning in the late 1960s and early 1970s, the study of what was alternatively labeled "government coercion" (i.e., arrests), "coercive capacity" (i.e., security force size), and "negative sanctions" (i.e., censorship) was initiated with a few conceptual pieces, a decent number of historical case studies and a few quantitative evaluations. By the late 1980s and early 1990s, many things had changed: the labels had shifted to "government terror," "political repression," as well as later "human rights violation," the behavior of interest was shifted to political arrests, torture as well as mass killing, and the sheer number of pieces increased dramatically—especially with regard to the number of quantitative investigations (the focus of the current research).[15]

In many respects, this literature has continued to grow and it has improved dramatically from how it began. For example, it is now much clearer what researchers are talking about when the topic is referenced (Davenport (2007) and Davenport and Inman (2012)); it is now much clearer how such behavior is measured (Wood and Gibney (2010)); it is now much clearer what is wrong with the indicators used and what could be done to improve them (Fariss (2014) and Ball (1996)); and, it is now much clearer how to systematically evaluate compiled data (Hill and Jones (2014); Conrad and Moore (2010); Ritter and Conrad (2016); Appel (2018); Blanton (1999); DeMeritt (2015); Hafner-Burton (2008); Hafner-Burton (2005); and Bueno de Mesquita et al. (2005)). Note that what has been mentioned thus far

---

[15] We start with the literature on government repression and not genocide/politicide, atrocities and the like for we view these behaviors as subsets of the broader category—government repression. By adopting the broader framing, we are better able to understand the larger-scale applications of repressive behavior but also maintain a comparison to other government action which is generally myopically focus on genocide/politicide and atrocity. In addition to this, there has been a greater amount of theoretical development undertaken in the repression literature as well as more detailed development of data and empirical estimation.

The Death and Life of State Repression: Understanding Onset, Escalation, Termination, and Recurrence.
Christian Davenport and Benjamin J. Appel, Oxford University Press. © Oxford University Press 2022.
DOI: 10.1093/oso/9780197655375.003.0002

as improvements to the literature are largely methodological in nature. In many respects, the literature has essentially been frozen in its theoretical conception of why repression is applied and the field has adopted a particular explanation of the relevant phenomenon that dominates this line of inquiry effectively squeezing/crowding out all competitors and, we will argue, complexities.[16] To date, generally some version of a cost-benefit analysis has been used where authorities consider diverse elements, weigh their relative importance, make a decision about whether or not to apply repression and (if selected) move forward with its application. This theoretical predominance is important because it has influenced what researchers look for when they evaluate compiled data as well as how they look for it.

How well has the theory done in exploring the phenomenon of interest? In all honesty, we do not really know the answer to this question because it has not been asked. When considered, however, it is clear that the evidence in support of the argument is limited in large part because its operationalization has been underdeveloped. Additionally, it appears that alternative explanations seem a little better at addressing the puzzles that emerge from this work.

In an attempt to move existing literature forward, we review the argument, assess how well it has done, offer a critique and use this critique to develop a new theory for government repression which draws upon, but improves, prior work. This leads to new hypotheses, data and modeling.

1.2 The Standard Argument and Its Evaluation

After initial theorization on repressive behavior and reflecting a broader turn found throughout the social sciences, research on government repression has largely adopted some version of rational choice with varying degrees of adherence (revealing "thin" as well as "thick" versions). Essentially, this approach attempts to understand how and when governments work collectively in order to engage in arrests, torture, disappearances, and killing (Gurr 1986; Poe and Neal Tate 1994; Davenport 2007; Pierskalla 2010; Tyson 2018). At its core, the theory centers around an explicit evaluation of distinct

---

[16] This said, there have been a decent number of theoretical innovations in formal work but this has resulted in few empirical investigations beyond an isolated case or two.

actions that could be and later are taken by political authorities made within a specific period of time (e.g., a week or, more commonly, a year).

The factors considered within the theory fall into two primary and two secondary categories. The two primary components include what are referred to as "costs" and "benefits." The former involves those things that are lost from engaging in repressive action. Presumably paid by political authorities, this includes "political" costs such as losing office/power and being punished/sanctioned for using repression like when fines are paid or leader popularity is diminished. This also includes "operational" costs such as paying salaries to those who enact relevant behavior and forgoing different investments of government resources. In contrast, benefits refer to those things gained from engaging in repressive behavior. Again, presumably collected by those in political office, this would include establishing or increasing access to resources. We say "presumably" above because the recipient and good(s) delivered/obtained are never specified in too much detail within previous research.[17]

For the more sophisticated, nuanced, as well as rare investigations of state repression, there is consideration of another two (secondary) items: alternatives and a probability of success. As conceived, alternatives involve mechanisms of influence which do not rely upon coercion and force. For example, one could consider economic power such as bribes and the allocation of resources as well as normative power such as issuing directives and employing persuasive speech. The probability of success concerns an evaluation of how likely the repressive behavior being considered will be in achieving the desired end.

Taking all these factors into consideration, repressive behavior would be expected when benefits exceed costs, alternatives are not available, and the probability that repression would be successful is high. In contrast, repressive behavior would not be expected when costs exceed benefits, alternatives are readily available, and the probability of successful repression is low.

When one thinks about it, there are many ways that one could evaluate the quality of this argument with regard to its ability to explain repressive action. We consider numerous possibilities below.

---

[17] Older research also suggests that economic elites benefit from maintaining exploitative and highly profitable economic relations but this is less commonly mentioned in the last 10–15 years. Within this framework, repressive behavior is expected when benefits exceed costs. When the situation is reversed or when the two are viewed as being equal, repression is not expected. Importantly, the identification, collection and evaluation of these factors are conducted by a singular actor (government) across a designated time period (e.g., across nation-years).

1.2.1 On Its Own Merits

The first way to evaluate the rational theory of repression is with regard to conceptual clarity. Here, we explore whether the various elements of the argument are easily comprehended and reasonably employed. On this point, existing research is found to be very much wanting.

Let's initially consider the primary categories. As conceived, it is not exactly clear what actor should be (and is) assessed for costs. Is it the individual politician who initially puts together the broad objectives to be pursued? Is it a particular cohort of political leaders or the whole government? Is it the impact of costs on security force agents that are the ones to be evaluated? Should one consider politicians and/or security force agents together? Is it the costs directed against the economic elite that provides the parameters within which repressive objectives and policies are constructed, like suggested in largely forgotten literatures on dependency and world system theory? Relatedly, who benefits from repression? Is it possible that different actors benefit from repressive behavior and that the different actors should be considered at the same time?

Other questions exist as well. For example, how should researchers juxtapose costs against benefits? How much of a specific benefit offsets a specific cost or multiple costs? How many costs (e.g., naming/shaming, leading to a loss of perceived legitimacy in the international community, threat/imposition of economic sanctions, removal from office via the vote in an election) and how many benefits (i.e., prioritized access to government resources and exemption from taxation) should be evaluated at the same time? We know very little about these questions and they are all crucial to investigate for the field to advance.

Considering the secondary categories outlined above (i.e., alternatives and probability of success), additional questions emerge. For example, are all alternatives for political authority equally likely to be employed or even thought of across contexts? Should those interested in studying state repression move away from a more passive conceptualization of the way that decisions are made given that security force agents are believed to be intentionally and consistently lobbying for their use on a consistent basis? What is the impact of such lobbying and does it offset the lobbying efforts of those championing material and normative power?

Part of the difficulty with answering these questions concerns the fact that the different mechanisms of influence wielded by distinct actors are associated with literatures that do not generally consider one another. For instance, literature on government repression rarely considers alternative mechanisms of control/influence beyond democracy and economic cooptation/development. Other literatures aren't much better as research on coup-proofing and how security forces are treated rarely considers government repression. Even when these alternatives are incorporated, very little attention is given to how they function.

A second way to evaluate the predominant rationalist theory is with regard to operational clarity. Here, again, we see some difficulties. For example, when one attempts a straightforward mapping of the primary categories to be evaluated (i.e., costs and benefits) onto the variables generally used in estimated models (e.g., democracy, civil war, population, naming/shaming, military intervention, and so forth) complexities immediately arise. Historically, researchers don't seem to have much of a difficulty coming up with costs: i.e., economic sanctions, naming/shaming, military intervention, holding elections, and signing/ratifying human rights treaties would readily be identified. Indeed, these are among the most readily available as well as consistently made arguments in the literature. All variables have seemingly straightforward connections to things that political authorities and security force agents would like to avoid. This said, some variables just don't seem to fit within designated categories. For example, GDP per capita offers a distinct mechanism of control (involving an alternative) but one can also make the case that it also provides resources to governments (involving a cost). This mirrors the variable uses of GDP within the literature concerned with civil war where it alternatively serves as a measure of capacity for the government or economic opportunity for citizens.

Other problems exist with the standard decision calculus as well. For example, it is unclear across what time horizon it makes sense to evaluate costs and benefits. Should one consider 1 year, 5 years, 10 years, or 20 years? It is (again) not clear.

1.2.2   Explanatory Power

A different way to evaluate the predominant theoretical framework is to consider how well it accounts for repression when it is examined. The logic here would be that if repressive behavior were explained consistently as well as thoroughly (presuming variables could be associated with the different parts of the standard explanation addressed above), then we could at least know that we were moving in the right direction of generally accounting for the phenomenon of interest.

At first glance, the existing empirical models appear to do quite well as several of the variables that are easily fit into the designated categories above prove to be statistically as well as substantively important. But, as noted above, there are some variables that do not easily fit within existing theory and/or which are not consistently supported by empirical examinations. This introduces some complexity.

For example, there is a core set of variables that are found to be statistically significant as well as substantively important on a consistent basis. One of the variables most associated with government repression (generally viewed as a [if not] the cost) is political democracy. Consistent with the predominant approach, however it is measured (i.e., election, executive constraint, veto points, party representativeness, judicial independence, media openness), this variable consistently decreases human rights violation. Now, it is clear that researchers could be better about evaluating distinct aspects of democracy within the same piece, rather than simply examining particular ones (e.g., executive constraints) or adopting some index that combines different aspects together (e.g., like Polity). Research could also be better at explaining the causal mechanisms involved. Is it toleration or fear that motivates political leaders, and who is feared—the citizens or the security apparatus? Regardless, the repeated identification of the same empirical finding across studies compels acknowledgment that there is something there.

Another variable (behavioral challenge) consistently increases state repression. Consistently, different types and levels of repressive behavior are increased in the face of political dissent, terrorism as well as insurgency.[18] In many ways, this research is developed. For instance, the mechanism of influence here is comparatively much clearer than that concerning democracy.[19] In others it is not well developed. For example, are behavioral challenges best thought of as a benefit to political authorities when reduced? This is unclear.

Variables associated with particular contextual factors have also been consistently identified. As one example, population size (potentially a cost as larger groupings are harder to manage) is always identified as a positive influence on government repression. Additionally, more recent research has

[18] The first finding has been somewhat tainted because researchers have generally forgotten that civil war involves both challengers as well as governments in the concept. To say that one form of repression is relevant to another generally makes little sense.

[19] Regardless, the stability in empirical findings is unmatched in the literature.

revealed that youth bulges (potentially a cost as well because larger cohorts present greater potential threat) tend to increase repressive behavior.

Outside of the core variables identified above, however, there are a variety of explanatory factors that (despite receiving a decent amount of attention) have received mixed empirical support: e.g., this includes treaties regarding international human rights, military intervention, naming/shaming, and economic sanctions. Revealing a particular focus of existing research, these are all typically understood as costs.

In addition to these less consistently supported explanatory factors, there are a host of policies/variables that have received very little or sporadic attention. For example, there is some earlier research on economic dependency (a potential benefit of repression as protection and profitable economic relations exist). This variable was always statistically significant and positive in its impact but it generally fell out of favor after the 1980s and was rarely examined after that point. There was research on military capacity and the involvement of the military in political systems which has recently re-emerged as a variable of interest in the examination of authoritarian types.[20] These two aspects of the phenomenon of interest concern the probability of success as greater military wherewithal would seem to promote effective application of coercion and force. A different variant of this work is focused on the existence and role played by government militias (Butler, Gluch, and Mitchell 2007). Lastly, there have been few evaluations of arms trading (Blanton 1999). Similar to the other variables being discussed, despite statistical significance this measure and the arguments associated with it have never quite caught on and thus they have not been widely evaluated—at least, not yet.

1.2.3 Remaining Puzzles

A final way to evaluate existing theory is to consider what puzzles remain in the literature that seem unresolved/unresolvable within the predominant framework.

One such puzzle concerns an interesting series of findings which reveal that "domestic" factors (i.e., those which originate within the relevant territorial jurisdiction like electoral democracy/democratization, behavioral

---

[20] This second wave is more directly connected with the literature on political authorities as opposed to work more specifically on military institutions and military sociology.

challenges) generally seem to outweigh the importance of those that could be classified as "international" (e.g., those that originate outside of the relevant territorial jurisdiction like military intervention, naming/shaming, economic sanctions, and the signing/ratification of international treaties). Furthermore, among the domestic variables, empirical findings tend to favor political (e.g., diverse behavioral challenges, system type, and judicial independence) as well as demographic factors (e.g., population and youth bulge) over those that would be classified as economic in nature (e.g., GDP per capita). The question remains why.

The rationalist framing of existing work would suggest that domestic factors simply count/weigh more in the decision calculus but there has been no such argument put forward. Most research contains vague references to the decision calculus identified above as well as imprecise mappings from theoretical components to the variables contained in estimated models. In order for research in this area to get better and for solutions to government repression to be more readily available for those interested in the topic, however, there needs to be something offered theoretically in order to properly guide empirical work.

Related, a second puzzle concerns lagged repression which simultaneously sits as one of (if not) the most important variable considered within empirical studies of government repression in terms of statistical and substantive impact (Davenport 1995; Poe and Neal Tate 1994) as well as the variable that has received the least amount of theoretical attention. Lagged repression presents a puzzle for existing literature because it is not quite clear how the predominant theoretical model with its emphasis on repeatedly assessing collected (new) information is challenged/overwhelmed by considerations of what repressive practices have been used before. Indeed, this variable and its consistent impact tends to push against the underlying logic of the rationalist approach, leading in the direction of an alternative explanatory framework (discussed further below). This theoretical challenge is further magnified when it becomes clear that influences are not simply contemporaneous or simply a single year or two like that most commonly examined (Sullivan, Loyle, and Davenport 2012) but that the impact could extend back 10 years (Davenport 1996) or longer (Gurr and Lichbach 1986). When contemplated, these extended influences render a rationalist account of repression much less plausible.

The last puzzle presented by existing literature is equally troubling for those who adopt a rationalist approach. For example, a decent amount of research has been dedicated to examining the influence of state repression on behavioral challenges. While this work is generally not referenced in the research concerned with the determinants of government repressive action, it is clearly relevant as much of the literature is based on the argument that repression is used in order to keep challenges to a minimum as well as to keep authorities in office. Although the impact on survival has received hardly any empirical attention (see Escribà-Folch (2013) and Davenport, RezaeeDaryakenari, and Wood (2021) for exceptions), the impact on behavioral challenges has been examined extensively where it is revealed that governments are not really good at defeating protestors, terrorists, rebels, and/or insurgents. Some work finds that repressive behavior decreases such behavior but other work finds that repression increases these challenges or has no impact at all (Davenport 2007).

These mixed findings are puzzling because they suggest that one of the primary benefits of repressive behavior (i.e., threat reduction) is not only empirically unlikely but moreover it might actually make things worse for political authorities by increasing resistance/rebellion—impacting the likelihood of success. If repression does not diminish challenges, however, then why would it continue to be used, see Davenport and Loyle (2012) for interesting explanation of this question?

It is possible that we simply have the wrong objective/outcome in mind and that the rationalism discussed above could still be used. For example, it may be the case that the objective of government repression is to protect individual leaders and/or particular governments which is a common (i.e., albeit unexplored) assumption within existing research. While it is unclear about repression's ability to protect individual incumbents, given the relative stability of government over time, it appears that in this view repressive behavior is generally successful in keeping governments in power. It may be the case that political authorities are more interested in producing exploitative and unequal economic distributions like those highlighted within earlier research. By this criteria, with the small likelihood of inequality changing over time, again we find that the use of repressive behavior appears to be highly successful and thus its application makes sense.

While plausible, none of these arguments have been made in the literature concerned with rigorously investigating the phenomenon of interest. Indeed, a major problem lies in not subjecting these ideas regarding alternative objectives to empirical investigation. Without actual success (which points to the efficacious use of government repression), it would appear that the use of repressive behavior might not serve any purpose in the maximization of utility (i.e., there must be something maximized such as order [no challengers], stability [no change in institutions], and/or continued economic exploitation [no change in inequality]). This all sits as a rather large puzzle for existing work.

Related to this, there are some other theories which call into question the idea of repeatedly collecting information as well as evaluating and updating cost/benefit calculations to guide subsequent decision and behavior. For example, there are several arguments which maintain that the evaluations suggested in the rational framework are seldom made and/or done on a limited basis (e.g., consider "satisficing" or bounded rationality). This would go well with the finding that government repression is "sticky" and fairly stable in its application over time (Hafner-Burton (2005) and Gurr (1986)). The possibility of evaluation in line with predominant theory is further challenged by work referred to as "commitment escalation" (Staw 1981). Within this research, it is maintained that a decision calculus is undertaken at some point in a manner similar to that described above by rationalism but that this only happens at the beginning of the policy in question. After implementation, those involved with decision-making do not revisit their earlier calculation. Rather, they prevent opportunities for revisitation and adjustment. Indeed, if a circumstance does arrive for reflection, any opinion that is critical of the earlier decision is ignored or attacked. In contrast, any opinion that is supportive of the prior decision would be highlighted as well as advanced. Such a response is in part influenced by the fact that those involved with the earlier decision have become emotionally attached to it as well as the resulting policy. This would cause them to protect not only the earlier decision but also their identities which are subsequently associated with what was implemented.

1.3 The Juggernaut Theory of Repressive Spells

Although we agree with the basic idea of a decision calculus as well as the importance of raising costs in order to negatively impact government repression, we suggest moving away from the predominant rationalist approach applied within the literature. Indeed, we offer a different argument, which is provided below.

We begin with focusing our attention not on all repressive activity but only that which is large-scale and severe (i.e., violent). We do this for a variety of reasons. First, this is the behavior that has been the focus for most individuals and institutions who are concerned with human rights violation, genocide, atrocities and the like. This includes victims, ordinary citizens, activists, advocates, researchers, and politicians. Second, this is the behavior that has taken the largest number of lives among all forms of political conflict and violence since the creation of the modern nation-state. Third, we believe that behavior below this level is largely driven by different factors.

With this focus on large-scale, state repression, we argue that this behavior is essentially the end product of a three-part series:

(1) the thoughts, discussions and actions of political authorities who design the basic contours of the repressive policy to be implemented (i.e., what is the objective, who is the target and what tactics should not be employed);

(2) the thoughts, discussions and actions of the leaders of coercion/force-wielding institutions who work out the more specific details of the repressive effort laid out by political leaders (i.e., specifically what the rules of engagement will/can be as well as the allocation of duties); and,

(3) the actions of the repressive agents themselves who actually engage in beating, torture, and killing as well as the norms of practice (i.e., standard operating procedures) that develop after they have begun.

What is clear from this conception is that thousands and potentially millions of individuals as well as actions, distributed across the relevant territorial unit of interest, can be involved in the implementation of repression and that this "leviathan" (i.e., this immense, violence-wielding body) is the entity that begins to move, enacting the behavior of interest—the onset of the repressive spell.

At this stage in the life cycle of government repression, we maintain that concerned individuals should be focused on the creation of the repressive cohort (i.e., all of the individuals and institutions that come to be favorably disposed toward large-scale repressive behavior as a policy option). Viewed in this manner, we believe that relevant activity is influenced by factors pointed towards individuals within the relevant theoretical unit with little role being played by international ones. This differential effect is attributed to the fact that repression is largely driven by more proximate and localized forces which influence the relevant actors perceptions of what is going on as well as what should be done about it. This is not to say that more international forces like colonialism, imperialism, capitalism do not matter—especially as they influence conceptions of identity, perceived threat and the like but rather this is to acknowledge that repressive behavior involves activities within a specified territorial unit and time, largely being influenced by context-specific factors that are somewhat immediate and obvious.[21] To the degree that international forces can reinforce domestic forces (i.e., with resources, training, and/or personnel), we would expect international factors to be quite impactful.

We don't simply wish to prioritize domestic over international factors at the onset phase but we also wish to prioritize among domestic factors in order to highlight the ones that believed to be the most central to governance—i.e., some mechanisms of popular accountability (i.e., the level of electoral democracy and movements toward democracy/democratization), the rule of law (i.e., judicial aspects of democracy) as well as some conception of the need for repressive behavior (i.e., political threat such as political dissent, non-violent direct action, civil war, youth bulges, and population size). Again, while international factors are not believed to have much of a direct influence, we do believe that international factors could play an indirect role on influencing government.

This brings us to our second point. While it is useful to have the leviathan image in mind as one begins to think about the origins of large-scale, severe repression, once an LSSR is underway we would suggest that it is more accurate/appropriate to think of a "juggernaut" (i.e., a huge, powerful, and slowly moving entity). Once in motion, the repressive juggernaut is easily perturbed in an upwards fashion, leading to escalation. In this context, the repressive cohort has already made their evaluation in favor of coercion/force and mobilized to take such action. While individuals and institutions are not generally open to information and deliberation that move against the application of government repression, the relevant actors would be more than open and, indeed, would be looking for opportunities to reinforce decisions and dynamics that were already in place. As a consequence, we would expect political authorities in a spell to be hypersensitive to all threats both domestic (e.g., dissent, civil war, population, and youth bulges) and

---

[21] This is distinct from the ideas of "transnational" repression where domestic actions are driven by external actors. We don't feel that this would generally surpass domestic factors or actors in large-scale applications.

international (e.g., military intervention, economic sanction, naming/sham-ing, and international treaties). Here, it is important to note that what are conceptually believed to be costs as they punish and isolate political authorities are framed by political authorities as threats.[22] This prompts the cohort to further insulate and dig into earlier positions, reinforcing the application of government repression even further and facilitate what would be best characterized as benefits.

Although spells are generally easy to turn/ramp up, they are generally less easy to stop (i.e., terminate)—as discussed earlier this was our central concern initially and thus we will explicate the point here in some detail. Drawing on the work of Staw (1981), we maintain that after the initial cost-benefit analysis commonly discussed in the literature has been made and repression is implemented, the individuals and groups within the relevant process become connected to the decision on not only an organizational/bu-reaucratic level but also a psychological one. This prompts cohort members to do their best to avoid thinking of the prior decision negatively as this would reflect poorly on themselves as well as the process used to make the relevant decision. As Staw (1981) suggests:

> since it is difficult for the subject . . . to undo the consequences of (previ-ously undertaken activity), it is predicted that the individual (and group within which they exist) will bias (their) attitude on the . . . task . . . so as to cognitively reduce any negative outcomes resulting from (their) behavior. In short, the individual is predicted to justify (their) previous behavior or defend (themselves) from negative consequences through the perceptual biasing of behavioral outcomes.

This framework is important for a discussion of government repression because within it political authorities are not expected to objectively assess information coming to them regarding the relevant environment on a con-sistent basis and at clearly defined intervals. Rather, after the decision to repress has been made, the actors of interest are more likely to reduce the processing of new and potentially challenging information or ignore information entirely as they rely upon the people, perceptions, as well as policies that emerged leading up to the initial application of repressive action.

---

[22] This insight was first made by Kathman and Wood (2011) regarding military intervention but we believe it is generalizable to any external intervention as these all threaten sovereignty.

As long as the overall repressive process that initiated the relevant action remains intact, we expect such a position to be maintained.

Such an argument significantly deviates from previous work on government repression which generally conceives of the repressive process as one that can easily be switched against repression by introducing just the "right" cost (e.g., naming and shaming, threatening to impose economic sanctions or engaging in military intervention). This work presumes, however, that the selected cost-producing variable is sufficient to disturb what we have characterized as a juggernaut—something which we do not believe is true.[23]

The implication here is clear. Within our framework, relevant actors are not likely to change what they are doing and in order to figure out when a change in behavior is most likely to result, one must identify when the actors involved in the repressive process are effectively disrupted. This brings us back to the various cost-producing policies identified in the literature but, different from this work, we consider the differential impact and weight given to diverse policies simultaneously.

When we do this, of all factors believed to influence government repressive behavior, we maintain that it is democratization that is the most likely to exhibit an impact on spell termination. This is because increasing the level of democracy offers the most substantive disruption of the repressive process. Before getting there though, it is useful to clarify some concepts.

In our view, democracy (at its core) refers to a particular form of institutional arrangement where some constituency (i.e., group of citizens) selects another group of individuals to make decisions concerning the general direction of the relevant political unit. These relationships are structured in a way that political authorities are (theoretically) held accountable to the constituency that lives within the territorial jurisdiction of interest. Exactly how leaders are chosen, how accountability is established, how active the different actors are varies across researchers but the concept is associated with a more bottom-up orientation and it involves a particular set of actors and actions.

For example, some scholars focus on the existence of elections (as we do in this book), maintaining that this is the principal means by which citizens

---

[23] This is also differentiated from Principal Agent arguments which tend to highlight the important role of individualistic/selfish motives of agents and their defection from the directives of principals. We see these as being more appropriate for lower-level/scale repressive behavior or isolated events than LSSR.

select who governs and, through this activity, make their political leaders accountable. Here, those countries that have elections are believed to be more democratic than those that do not. Some focus on what percentage of the population has an opportunity to participate in the selection of political leaders. The argument here is fairly straightforward as the degree of democracy held by a country (i.e., the representative nature of leadership selection and the magnitude of accountability found in the country) would be reflected by how much of the nation-state participated in the leaders selection. Some focus on political parties. Here, it is important that the organizations broadly represent the relevant population contained within the polity of interest (i.e., capturing the diversity of beliefs and/or demographic categories). The broader the amount of people with political representation, the more democratic the government would be. Some focus on executives and the underlying concern here lies in the degree to which an executive is compelled to consider diverse opinions and/or be subject to them in a systematic fashion through counselors, advisors, and rival/independent organizations of power. If an executive has to consider no one else's opinion and they are completely insulated from them, then this would be considered a relatively nondemocratic executive. If, however, an executive has to consider the opinion of others and they can be overruled or blocked by these others in some way, then the system would be considered a relatively more democratic one. The specific actors involved in facilitating monitoring and accountability include the media where it is maintained that if this actor exists and they are relatively independent from those in control, then the executive is better countered and more likely to be in a situation where one could classify a democracy. Some highlight the existence of an independent judiciary (which we do in this book as well) for similar reasons.

The discussion of the different actors/actions is crucial to identify for shifts in any single aspect or several at the same time regarding the direction of democracy represent what we call "democratization." As Ulfelder and Lustik (2007) instruct us "democratic transitions can take many different forms and follow many different paths." Indeed, these differences have led to a robust literature focusing on the different institutions/practices identified above. This variability has important implications for the selection of our democratization measure, the empirical tests that we use and the interpretations of the findings (discussed below).

In contrast to democracy and democratization with its bottom-up orientation, state repression refers to a particular type of government behavior that is enacted by the designated agents of said authority who directly hold/maintain coercive and forceful power within the relevant territorial unit (i.e., the security forces). The actors that one focuses on here can vary (e.g., the police, military, militias, intelligence organization, or special forces) along with the behavior that one highlights (e.g., spying, arrests, beating, torture, disappearance, and killing). Regardless, the general concept is associated with a more top-down orientation and it involves a different set of actors as well as actions than generally thought of with regard to democracy and democratization. The discussion above is important, for we argue that movements toward democracy (i.e., democratization) represent a disruptive change to the repressive cohort and process noted above (i.e., the actors involved, the relationships that exist, the policies advanced, and the policies implemented).

Now, more "maximalist" conceptions of democracy tend to conflate these two processes together (whereby mechanisms of selection/accountability as well as favored coercive/forceful policies are identified). Our approach is more "minimalist" in nature because in line with diverse theorists, policy-makers, activists, and citizens, we view democracy as simply a mechanism of selection and potential accountability, which we believe might have important behavioral aftereffects. Such a position allows us to gauge the impact of the institutional arrangement on government behavior, avoiding tautology. Our approach is also more in line with existing quantitative literature where it has been shown that the influence of political democracy and democratization on variations within government repression has been anything but straightforward and linear (Davenport and Armstrong (2004); Hill (2016); Lupu (2013a)).

We maintain that the shift in political systems has significant implications for the repressive juggernaut described above. For example, with new leader-ship and mechanisms of accountability put in place, democratization leads to transformations in who occupies positions of power and following this it leads to changes in the policies these leaders pursue in government as well as how they train, arm and issue commands related to repression in particular—especially of a lethal, widespread, and systematic manner. Indeed, it is in part through highlighting the differences from the previous regime that the newly democratized government distinguishes itself from the authority it replaces. Shifting repressive practices is one way to achieve this end.

Not only might the policymaking aspect of the repressive process be altered following democratization but the willingness of the agents of atrocity to comply with directives they were provided with changes as well. Acknowledging the new "will of the people" in the selection of leaders, coercive/forceful agents within democratizing contexts withdraw from their participation in the repressive juggernaut out of fear that they could invite rebellion and/or diminish support/resource allocations for themselves in the new context.

In short, unlike the diverse international factors noted above which have to work through shifting the opinions of actors already involved in repressive decision-making and implementation (which we identified as being difficult to do because of the institutional and psychological attachment to the relevant policy), democratization works directly through replacing decision-makers outright and/or fundamentally altering the way that they are selected as well as potentially held accountable. Additionally, democratization indirectly prompts repressive agents to reduce repression by shifting the chain of command between principal and agent, the basis for political legitimacy held by leaders as well as the perception of popular accountability maintained by all involved with the political system.

Now, as LSSRs begin with threats, one might think that spells would end with changes in behavioral challenges but we do not believe this to be the case. Indeed, while we maintain that threat perception is grounded/initiated in something real, once these characteristic features become institutionalized into policy and practice, they develop a life of their own with relevant political authorities. And, because of the bureaucratic inertia and identity infused with this initial perception, after being assembled it is not easy to talk politicians "off this ledge"/out of this concern. This leaves us with understanding recurrence.

While in many respects it would seem appropriate to suggest that these contexts would be similar to those that precede the onset of LSSR, this would be ignoring the fact that the use of large-scale, severe repression has an impact on the governments and societies that they take place within. As such, we do not anticipate similar causal factors for those found relevant to onset. Indeed, we expect very few factors to be systematically related to this phenomenon. Suffering from a version of "war-weariness" we would argue that most nation-states that have had an LSSR previously are not likely to have another but if there are repeat offenders, most likely this results from inadequate movement beyond the repressive cohort that existed during the last LSSR.

Such a realization would again point us in the direction of specific domestic factors. For example, democratization should play a role as this signals some disturbance to the repressive leviathan[24] in line with the discussion above. Some degree of economic development might provide political authorities with an alternative mechanism of control which would undermine the necessity for coming forward with a more coercive/forceful solution to the problem of socio-political order.

It is useful not only to identify what we believe will have an impact but also to identify what we believe will not. For example, we do not believe that most aspects of the international community will play much of a role in situations of recurrence because (like onset) this stage of the repressive process is very much an internal affair. This said, it is possible that some international factors play a role. For example, some suggest that extensive "boots on the ground" might hinder political authorities from returning to behavior associated with the previous government. We highlight this particular policy because of the direct way that it is believed to impact potential implementation.

---

[24] As repression had terminated, the juggernaut is now once again back to its pre-movement incarnation.

2

Studying Spells: A New Unit of Analysis, Measure, and Model

2.1 Introduction

In order to examine what influences the various aspects of the repressive life cycle identified above (i.e., onset, escalation, duration/termination, and recurrence), we had to find or generate data that allowed us to measure our new conception. Toward this end, we created a global data set of large-scale, severe repression (LSSR) spells which we defined as the duration of time government behavior existed above a certain threshold (i.e., a particular level of severity and size of the targeted population). When repression moves above this threshold, a spell begins. As long as repressive action stays above this level, it continues. Once repression falls below the designated level, the spell terminates. And, if, after having gone through a spell already, repressive behavior once again rises above the designated threshold, it is said to recur.

Within the current study, the threshold used to determine when a spell has occurred (or not) was derived from the Political Terror Scale (hereafter PTS). To date, this database sits as the most popular indicator of state repression in existing scholarship, one of the most valid comparative/global indicators of political conflict/violence available and arguably the most relevant to our discussion of spells as it simultaneously addresses the lethality of state behavior enacted as well as the scope of the population being targeted (Wood and Gibney 2010).

As conceived, PTS defines its behavior of interest as being "violations of physical or personal integrity rights carried out by a government (or its agents) ... and includes abuses such as extrajudicial killing, torture or similar physical abuse, disappearances, and political imprisonment" (Wood and Gibney 2010, p. 5). Put differently, the PTS measures the levels of "government terror" practiced domestically by a particular government and its affiliates for every country in the world against those who reside within

The Death and Life of State Repression: Understanding Onset, Escalation, Termination, and Recurrence.
Christian Davenport and Benjamin J. Appel, Oxford University Press. © Oxford University Press 2022.
DOI: 10.1093/oso/9780197655375.003.0003

their territorial jurisdiction in a yearly basis.[25] The sources used for these data include reports published by Amnesty International (AI) and the United States Department of State (USDS) which are used to create two distinct measures. More recent years also consider Human Rights Watch. In line with standard practice, we use the PTS measure based on Amnesty International's annual reports on human rights but we use the State Department data to fill-in missing values on the former.

Regarding the codings themselves, the AI and USDS variables range from 1 to 5. In level 1, those within the relevant territorial domain are generally not imprisoned for their political views and situations of political torture, beatings, and murder are rare/isolated. In level 2, state-sponsored coercion and force may occur but they are very limited in scope and lethality. Within the third level of the PTS, there is extensive political imprisonment and detention, execution, and other political murders as well as brutality are common. A score of 4 on PTS indicates that the behavior noted above has expanded to larger numbers of the population. Finally, a score of 5 represents an environment where government coercion and force has spread to the whole population.

Based on these definitions and given our interest with LSSR, the threshold used to identify spells is centered around when PTS is scored 3 and above. This coding rule is consistent with prior academic work that looks at government repression in the "worst" situations (e.g., Hafner-Burton 2005). There is also face validity to using 3 and above to create the LSSR spells. Comparing our list to the genocide/politicide data compiled by the Political Instability Task Force (e.g., Harff 2003), we find that all genocides/politicides since 1976 can be found within LSSRs measured in this manner.[26]

With these coding rules, the data is structured in such a way that once a country reaches PTS=3, the country is considered to be undergoing a repressive spell (i.e., onset begins). The number of years at PTS 3 (or above) constitutes the duration of the spell. This spell continues until the PTS drops below 3 for at least two consecutive years[27] at which point it is designated as terminated. A complete list can be found in the Appendix at the end

---

[25] These scores only reflect human rights violations committed by the government or its agents. They do not account for gangs, insurgent groups, or other non-government actors who may have political motivations.

[26] Alternative cut offs have been evaluated and our general findings hold. This increases our confidence in the measurement strategy selected.

[27] We felt that a single year was likely inviting too many problems as they could easily be attributed to some kind of measurement effort.

of the book.[28] To illustrate our measurement, we briefly discuss Zimbabwe from 1980 through 1987 which constitutes the full duration of a spell in this country.

In 1979, Zimbabwe had no score on the PTS for it was not yet a country. At this time, it was under British rule and thus it did not yet have control over its government. In April of 1980, Zimbabwe achieved independence and at this time it received a PTS score of 3 meaning that it initiated a spell. Presumably this was done to assist the new government with establishing and maintaining order. In response to diverse threats from behavioral challenges (i.e., an uprising in Entumbane in 1980, a 1981 uprising in Glenville [PTS=3] as well as an alleged plot to initiate civil war in 1982 [PTS=3]), the LSSR continued—including extensive political imprisonment, regular political murders, and unlimited detention for political views. This environment worsened over the next few years as civil and political rights violations for those participating in politics increased alongside state-sponsored murders, disappearances, and torture. In 1984, the spell escalated to its zenith (PTS=5) when government-violence spread to the whole population. This time was characterized by a wide variety of violent activities being employed by the government against large swaths of the Zimbabwean population. The designation of especially violent behavior makes sense here because in 1984 the "Matabeleland genocide" or "Gukurahundi" hit its highest point with the systematic persecution of the Zimbabwe African People's Union (ZAPU) and all that were believed to be associated with them, a category which was not always clear. These activities and many of those undertaken at this time were perpetrated by then prime minister Robert Mugabe's Fifth Brigade in the Ndebele regions (comprised of soldiers drawn from a special unit of former Zimbabwe African Nationalist Liberation Army personnel which had fought together during the battle for independence). The outcome of this behavior was devastating, with approximately 20,000 deaths as well as the detention of an untold number in an exhaustive search for potential challengers to the government.[29] After 1984, repression diminished a bit in severity (moving to PTS level 4 in 1985 and 3 in 1986 as well as 1987) but as the codes post-1984 were above a 3 on the PTS scale, the spell was still underway. By 1988, however, the PTS score fell to a level of 2 and, achieving this value, the spell was over (i.e., it was terminated). Another spell takes

---

[28] We also include figures in the appendix to further illustrate when LSSR spells begin and end.
[29] The unit was unique not only in its composition but also in that it reported directly to Mugabe.

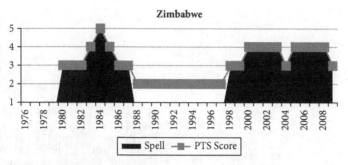

Fig. 2.1 Zimbabwe

place ten years later (in 1998) but this is a different campaign and thus beyond the scope of the current discussion.

2.2 Spells: The Dependent Variable

With some understanding of what we mean by a spell, in the following section we present some summary statistics on the dependent and independent variables employed within our empirical investigation. This is done to illustrate some of the key trends in the data and to provide some general understanding of what we are working with. Our discussion begins with the different dependent variables.

2.2.1 Large-Scale, Severe Repression
Spells—Overall Observations

Based on the coding rules identified above, our research identifies 244 spells from 1976–2006 that span all regions of the world. Within these data, the average duration of an LSSR spell is 10 years with a minimum length of one year and a maximum length of 32 years.

In Figure 2.2, we plot the number of ongoing spells by year. The graph clearly shows an increasing trend since 1976 (the first year of our study). In particular, there were 61 large-scale, severe spells in 1976, but this number increased to 98 spells in 2006.[30] Despite numerous efforts to prevent, lessen

---

[30] The 61 spells in 1976 represent spells that were ongoing as of 1976.

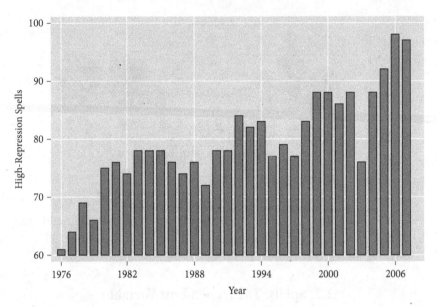

Fig. 2.2 LSSR Spells, 1976–2006

the severity of, and terminate LSSR spells as well as a significant amount of attention given to the alleged decline in other forms of political violence (not including state repression reported by scholars such as Pinker (2011)), we observe that LSSRs have not only continued to persist over the 30 years of our study but they actually grow in number![31]

Finally, we present a map that shows how long each country was involved in an LSSR (Figure 2.3). Within the figure, darker areas equate to more spell years in the country, while lighter ones represent fewer years. From the image, we see that 22 governments have been involved in LSSRs for basically the entirety of the time span under consideration (31 years), while 31 governments have used LSSRs for at least 23 years. Taken together, this suggests that over the 30 years of interest almost one-third of countries in the world routinely engaged in the worst forms of repression. This again seems to indicate how difficult it is to end spells, as evidenced by how many governments remain in them for long periods of time. On the other hand, we see that 34 countries have never engaged in LSSR, and 20 governments have employed LSSRs for less than six years. Finally, we observe important varia- tion by region. For example, both Africa and the Middle East are dominated

[31] Of course, this trend reflects the number of ongoing spells plus the onset of new spells. For additional evidence against declinism logic see Braumoeller (2019).

High-Repression Spell Duration

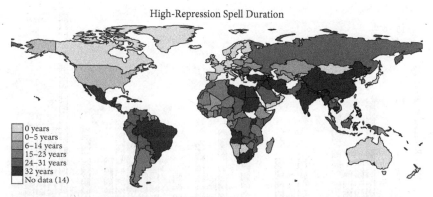

Fig. 2.3 Worldwide Duration of LSSR Spells

with governments in large-scale, severe repression spells, while we observe fewer governments in the Americas during the period of investigation.

2.2.2 Large-Scale, Severe Repression Spell Onset

As noted above, we conceptualize the beginning of an LSSR spell (our first dependent variable) as the initial year that a government reaches or surpasses a 3 on the PTS scale. To code this measure, we created a binary variable that equals 1 the first year that PTS codes a government a 3 or greater, and zero otherwise. In our data, there are 244 large-scale, severe repression spell onsets from a total of 2,666 observations from 1976 to 2006 (or around 10 percent of cases).[32] Spell onsets per year vary between 2 to 16 with a mean of about 6.[33]

In Figure 2.4, we graph the onset of LSSR spells across the entire time span of our data. While there is important variation, we see that spell onsets largely vary between 5 to 10 new onsets per year with a few years experiencing only a few onsets. Interestingly, we observe that governments started at least one spell every year in the data; in other words, there is not a single year where at least one government somewhere in the world refrained from initiating large-scale repression against those within their territorial domain.

[32] We drop cases of ongoing spells from the analysis, given our interest in the onset of such spells.
[33] This number excludes the first year in our data when 61 governments were already involved in LSSR spells.

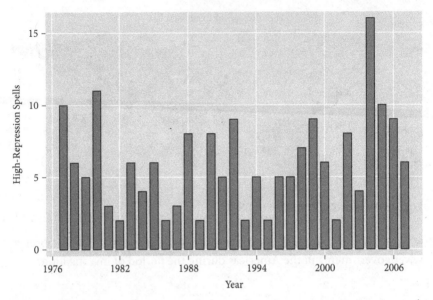

Fig. 2.4 Onset of LSSR Spells, 1976–2006

2.2.3 Large-Scale, Severe Repression Spell Escalation

For our second dependent variable (escalation), we analyze levels of repression within ongoing LSSR spells. This is done because governments, even in the context of high-level, sustained coercive and forceful behavior, can choose how much they want to repress those within their territorial jurisdiction and those interested in keeping repression as low as possible (even when LSSRs are underway) would be interested in this phenomenon. As a result, we look to see what factors are associated with the escalation (or de-escalation) of repression amidst an LSSR spell.

To that end, we create a three-category response variable that ranges from 3 to 5 in the PTS scale with larger values on the index indicating higher levels of repressive behavior. Within this conception, there are 2,539 observations (i.e., spell years) across the 244 spells in this stage of the repressive life cycle.

From our data, the average level of repression within a spell is about 3.5, with the minimum being 3 and the maximum at 5. In Figure 2.5, we plot the average values of this variable per year from 1976 to 2006. Here, we can see that for most years repressive behavior varies between 3.3 and 3.7, suggesting that governments on average repress at about a 3 on PTS—the lower end of the scale.

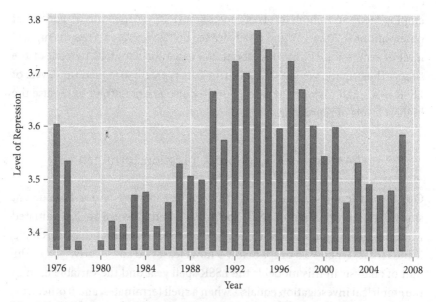

Fig. 2.5 Escalation of LSSR in LSSR Spells, 1976–2006

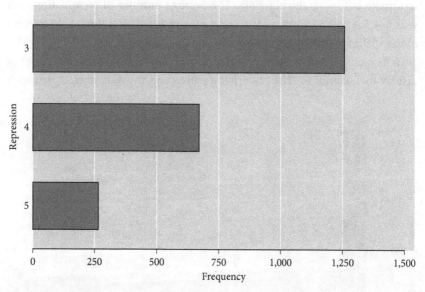

Fig. 2.6 Distribution of LSSR in LSSR Spells, 1976–2006

In Figure 2.6, we plot the distribution of this variable across LSSR spells. Consistent with earlier discussion, we observe that governments employ large-scale, severe repression at medium levels (PTS=3) 57 percent of the time (or in about 1,200 observations). Further, we see that governments employ medium to high levels of repression (PTS=4) in about 31 percent of observations (670 cases), and finally we see that governments use the highest level of repression (PTS=5) in about 265 cases (or about 12 percent of the time). Thus, again, we see that governments typically use medium levels of LSSR in a small majority of cases, but they also are not afraid to the use the highest levels of repression.

2.2.4 Large-Scale, Severe Repression Termination

Our third variable of interest and the original inspiration for the current study is the termination of LSSR spells. As noted above, a spell is initiated when a government receives a 3 or more on the PTS scale and, by this logic, it ends (dies) when PTS drops below 3 for at least two consecutive years. The unit of analysis in this model is the LSSR spell year and the variable used in the empirical investigation equals 1 when a spell terminates, and 0 otherwise. Seen in the figure below, among the 244 spells in our data, 145 (or 60 percent) terminate before or during 2006. The average number of terminations per year is 4.5 with a minimum of 1 and a maximum of 17. Of note, 40 percent of the spells we investigate do not end for the period we evaluate.

In Figure 2.7, we present a histogram of the repressive spells to better display their duration. The underlying patterns in the data suggest that spell

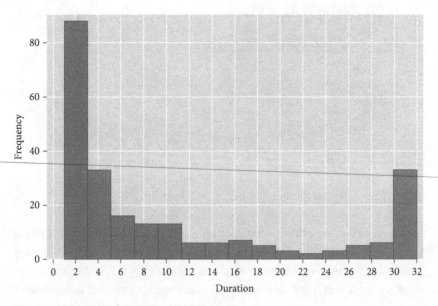

Fig. 2.7 Duration of LSSR Spells, 1976–2006

duration is largely bimodal; over 35 percent of spells terminate in less than three years, while over 30 percent of spells last over 20 years. We see that while many spells end in a few years, the majority of spells (over 65 percent) endure for at least five years. This is consistent with our larger argument that spells are sticky and it is difficult to terminate one after it has begun. It also suggests that very different explanations might exist for the different types of spells.

Related to this, it is interesting to compare the raw PTS scores across different spell lengths (speaking to the issue of levels and escalation above). For example, spells that terminate in less than three years receive scores of 4 or 5 on the PTS scale only 10 percent of the time. Ones that last longer than three years however engage in very severe repression (4 or 5) over 40 percent of the time. The data thus suggests that short-term spells consist of relatively mild forms of repression that are compared to more grave forms of repressive behavior that endure for much longer!

In Figure 2.8, we plot the number of governments that terminate spells. Here, we see that about 6 LSSR spells terminate every year with a minimum of one per year and a maximum of 20 in a single year (2002). Interestingly, with the exception of 2002, we do not see any increasing trend in terminations. This is somewhat surprising, given how much attention the

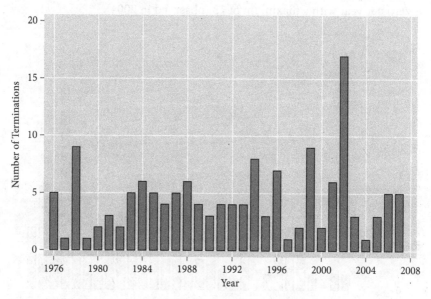

Fig. 2.8 Number of LSSR Spell Terminations, 1976–2006

international community—IGOs, NGOs, and third-party governments—has paid to ending large-scale atrocities, such as LSSR spells. This also deviates from research of "declinists" (like Steven Pinker) who argue that violence is diminishing over time.

2.2.5 Large-Scale, Severe Repression Recurrence

The fourth and final variable of interest (recurrence) equals 1 when an LSSR spell begins after one has already terminated, and zero otherwise. Here, the unit of analysis is the post-LSSR spell government year. In our data, spells recur 101 times, the average number of spell recurrences is 3 per year with a minimum of zero and maximum of 13 recurrences in a year. Overall, we see that spell recurrence is a very common phenomenon: over 40 percent of spells recur in our data, clearly indicating that recurrence is a major problem in the world!

In Figure 2.9, we plot the number of spell recurrences by year. Consistent with the onset data, we observe an increasing trend in the number of recurrences over the past 30 years. In particular, while we see that about 3 spells recur every year during this time span, most years see between 1 to 5 recurrences. Further, we see that the minimum number of recurrences is zero per year with a maximum of 13 (observed in 2004).

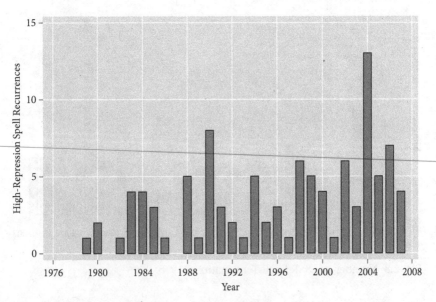

Fig. 2.9 LSSR Spell Recurrence, 1976–2006

2.3 Independent Variables

Consistent with the discussion of the literature, we include three categories of explanatory variables that are believed to impose costs on the repressive process: domestic factors, international factors, and domestic-international hybrids.[34] Each is discussed in turn below.[35]

2.3.1 Domestic Variables

Electoral Aspects of Democracy: In line with the domestic democratic peace proposition (Davenport 2007; Hill and Jones 2014; Bueno de Mesquita et al. 2005; Lupu 2013a; Davenport and Armstrong 2004), we include a measure for the level of democracy as described by Cheibub, Gandhi, and Vreeland (2010) that proxies electoral aspects of democracy. Discussed earlier, we use a minimalist indicator of democratic governance from Przeworski et al. (2000). Here, a regime is classified as a democracy if it meets four conditions: (1) the population or a popularly elected body must select the executive; (2) the legislature must be popularly elected; (3) there must be at least two parties participating in the elections; and, (4) when there is alternation (i.e., an incumbent executive is replaced by new executive via elections) the electoral rules must be identical to the ones that brought the incumbent to power in the first place. The variable used in the analysis equals 1 if the government is a democracy based on these rules, and zero otherwise. Following the large literature on this topic, we expect that democratic governments will be less likely to initiate large-scale, severe repression spells, see lower levels of escalation within ongoing spells, be more likely to terminate them once they have begun and less likely to have them recur.[36]

Electoral Democratization: Following Cheibub, Gandhi, and Vreeland (2010), this variable equals 1 in the year that the regime changes from a dictatorship to a democracy plus five additional years as long as the government remains a democracy. For example, if a government

---

[34] We include a table of summary statistics in the appendix at the end of this chapter.

[35] We lag all independent variables one year unless otherwise noted.

[36] It is important to note that our minimalist measure of democracy is independent from our measure of government repression that operationalizes government terror (i.e., terrorism, extrajudicial killings, etc.). As a result, there should be no concerns that our independent and dependent variables capture similar concepts.

democratized in 1990, the variable is coded a 1 in years 1990 through 1995.[37] We anticipate similar pacifying influences to those discussed by Davenport and Armstrong (2004).

Judicial Aspects of Democracy: Drawing on older theories of political democracy, recent literature suggests that domestic rule of law and in particular an independent judiciary imposes an important cost on political authorities. We therefore include Keith's rule of law measure that equals 1 for governments with complete de facto judicial independence and zero otherwise (Keith, Tate, and Poe 2009b). Drawing on recent research (Hill and Jones 2014), we expect that governments with strong rule of law systems will be less likely to start LSSR spells, escalate them, terminate them as well as restart them.[38]

2.3.2 International Variables[39]

Sticks: In this section, we identify costs that are generally labeled as "sticks" in international relations—some coercive/forceful behavior that is intended to induce compliance from the target government. The most prominent in the literature and public policy circles are discussed below but it is clear that the influence of these factors is less than clear. It is hoped that our consideration of the different parts of the repression life cycle will provide some insight into when and how the relevant policies/variables matter.

Military Interventions: In many respects, we begin with the international variable that most would probably think of when they think about how to negatively impact state repression. To measure this variable, we use Kisangani and Pickering's update of the Pearson and Baumann international

---

[37] As a robustness check, we assess the impact of all leadership changes as as well as autocratization on LSSR spells instead of democratization. Both measures were not statistically significant, indicating that only particular leader/regime changes such as those that produce democracies are associated with LSSR onset, termination, and recurrence.

[38] We also estimate robustness checks using the judicial independence variable based on the work of Linzer and Staton (2015). The results are consistent with those produced below. In addition, we examine the impact of movements towards greater domestic rule of law across the outcomes of interest, but we find no systematic support for this.

[39] We recognize that many scholars examine the relationship between naming and shaming and government repression. We exclude this variable from the results below due to missing data. As a robustness check, we include it in the models. The variable is not significant, and our results remain the same.

military interventions (IMI) data (Pickering and Kisangani 2009; Pearson and Baumann 1993). Following previous research (Wood, Kathman, and Gent 2012; Krain 2005) we focus on three types of interventions: (1) "pro-perpetrator"—where the intervention supports the government and/or opposes rebel/opposition groups when the perpetrator is the government, (2) "anti-perpetrator"—where the intervention opposes the government and/or supports the rebel/opposition groups when the perpetrator is the government and (3) "impartial"—where interventions are coded as non-supportive and/or neutral. We code a binary variable for each intervention type and lag these variables by one year in all models. While the literature has produced mixed findings on the relationship between interventions and government repression (Wood, Kathman, and Gent 2012; Krain 2005), we expect them to be associated with a lower probability of onset, escalation as well as recurrence and a higher probability of termination.[40]

Economic Sanctions: To code this variable, our study uses data from the Threat and Impositions of Sanctions (TIES) project (Morgan, Bapat, and Kobayashi 2014). As designed, we only include sanctions that are targeted at human rights violations and/or modifying contentious behavior related to conflict and repression undertaken by the government. Based on this, we create a binary variable, lagged one-year, that equals 1 when a third party enacts economic sanctions on a government, and zero otherwise. While some research finds that sanctions are linked with higher levels of repression (Wood 2008), we expect sanctions to decrease the likelihood of onset, escalation, and recurrence, as well as increase the probability of termination.

International Law: To code this variable, we rely on three human rights treaties that are widely discussed in the literature (Simmons 2009): the International Covenant on Civil and Political Rights (ICCPR), the Convention Against Torture (CAT), and The Convention on the Elimination of all Forms of Discrimination Against Women (CEDAW). In particular, we create a variable that is a count of the number of human rights treaties that each

---

[40] One could make militarization into a domestic-international hybrid because this variable begins internationally and then is imposed on some domestic setting but this differs from what we have in mind because we feel that it is the home or foreign nature of the variable that makes it either domestic or international. Additionally, we feel that intervention is one of the go-to policies of the international community with regards to dealing with LSSRs and choose to respect that orientation.

government has ratified. As such, the variable ranges from 0 to 3.[41] Although the literature finds mixed support for treaties (Appel 2018; Hill and Jones 2014; Lupu 2013b; Simmons 2009), we expect governments that have ratified the relevant treaties will be less likely to initiate the onset, escalation, and recurrence of LSSR repression as well as less likely to terminate it.

Carrots: Drawing upon existing literature, we also consider costs that are generally labeled as a "carrots"— i.e., some positive incentive that is intended to induce compliance from a targeted nation.

Preferential Trade Agreements (PTAs): To address this variable we include a measure that equals 1 if the government in question is a member of at least one PTA in a given year, and zero otherwise (Spilker and Böhmelt 2013; Mansfield and Milner 2012; Hafner-Burton 2005). Consistent with some recent research, we expect PTAs to be associated with a lower probability of onset and recurrence, lower likelihood of escalation as well as higher likelihood of termination.[42]

Intergovernmental Organizations (IGO) membership: Finally, we use data from Pevehouse, Nordstrom, and Warnke (2004) to capture government memberships in IGOs. This variable is a count of the total number of IGOs that each government is a formal member of in the current year. Consistent with existing argumentation, we expect IGO membership to be associated with a lower probability of onset and recurrence, lower likelihood of escalation as well as higher likelihood of termination.

2.3.3 Domestic-International Hybrids

While the policies/variables identified above are best understood as residing in the domestic or international communities there are a few variables which reside in both.

---

[41] Alternative coding rules for treaty membreship produce similar results.
[42] See however Spilker and Böhmelt (2013) for work that finds no relationship between PTAs and repression.

Civil Resistance: For example, we include in our analyses measures of civil resistance from the Nonviolent and Violent Campaigns and Outcomes (NAVCO) data project (Chenoweth and Lewis 2013). Consistent with our interests, we only include campaigns that target regime change or significant institutional reform (i.e., improve human rights practices). While using this variable, we acknowledged that there are both domestic as well as international versions of the indicator which allows us to assess whether this distinction is important. Accordingly, we created two variables.

The first variable equals 1 when the campaign in question did not receive any assistance from third-party actors (e.g., governments and IGOs), and zero otherwise. The second variable equals 1 when the campaign received third-party assistance and zero otherwise. Given research that suggests that nonviolence can be an effective tactic to engender policy change (Stephan and Chenoweth 2008; Chenoweth, Stephan, and Stephan 2011),[43] we expect these campaigns to be associated with a lower likelihood of onset, lower probability of escalation, higher probability of termination, and lower likelihood of recurrence.

International Nongovernmental Organization (INGO) Presence: To capture another domestic-international hybrid, we use a relatively new measure of International Nongovernmental Organizations (INGO) created by several scholars (e.g., Paxton, Hughes, and Reith 2015; Hughes et al. 2009). While this focuses on country-level interconnectedness, it also provides a useful way to measure INGO presence in governments, and consequently their impact on government behavior. As conceived, authorities with more connections to other governments in the international system interact with more INGOs. Consequently, these INGOs would have a greater opportunity to influence governments.[44] Assuming that the loss of the international connection introduces a cost to those subject to it, the INGO presence should reduce the likelihood of onset, escalation and recurrence while increasing the likelihood of spell termination.

---

[43] We recognize that campaigns may be associated with a higher probability of spell onset and escalation, as scholars find that leaders initially respond to civil resistance with higher levels of repression (Stephan and Chenoweth 2008; Chenoweth, Stephan, and Stephan 2011) Nonetheless, there are still good reasons to think that civil resistance may be negatively associated with the different phases of LSSR.

[44] Indeed, the authors of this measure argue that an INGO network is a better way to assess how INGOs influence government policy than merely a count of INGOs.

2.3.4 Control Variables

Looking back to the 1960s, these are some now-standard control variables that must be included in any serious investigation of state repression. We employ this group of variables within our study but we need to be clear: while employed widely in the study of state repression, the variables noted above have never been employed in an analysis of LSSR spells and thus it is possible that the effects differ between the different aspects of the repressive life cycle examined in this study. Each is discussed below.

Economic Development: Drawing on the earliest research on state repressive behavior, economic development is operationalized as GDP per capita based on purchasing power parity (Group 2014). In line with the existing literature (e.g., Hill and Jones (2014)), we expect governments with higher levels of economic development to be less likely to engage in LSSR, escalation, and the recurrence of it, as well as more likely to terminate it.

Population: Employing another measure used since the beginning of empirical repression studies and essentially every cross-national study of political behavior, we include the logged population of the government (lagged one year) (Henderson 1998; Group 2014). The expectation here is that logged population should be associated with higher probability of onset, escalation, and recurrence as well as a lower probability of termination.

Youth Bulges: Drawing on Nordås and Davenport (2013) as well as Hill and Jones (2014), we include a variable for youth bulges defined as "large cohorts in the ages 15–24 relative to the total adult population" (Urdal 2006, 608). Consistent with recent empirical work, we maintain that nation-states with relatively larger youth bulges are likely to see a higher probability of onset, escalation, recurrence, and a lower probability of spell termination.

Ongoing Civil War: In order to address large-scale behavioral challenges, our research includes a dummy variable for whether the government in question is involved in an ongoing "civil war". The measure uses the UCDP conflict data and is lagged one year. This equals 1 when a government is in a war (based on the 25 battle death threshold) and zero otherwise (Themnér and Wallensteen 2013). Consistent with the literature, we expect ongoing civil wars to be associated with a higher probability of spell onset, escalation, and recurrence as well as a lower likelihood of termination.

Civil War Termination: And last, to account for the end of civil war, we include a measure that equals 1 when a civil war ends and zero otherwise. Again, we use data from the UCDP/PRIO Armed Conflict dataset (Themnér and Wallensteen 2013) and we expect the onset, escalation, and recurrence of spells to be less likely following the end of a civil war, but that terminations will be more likely when this occurs.

2.3.5 Estimation Procedure

To test our theoretical argument on the different phases of the LSSR life cycle, we use multivariate regression analysis. This approach allows us to assess how a change in an independent variable of interest (i.e., democratization or economic sanctions) affects the dependent variable (e.g., LSSR onset, termination, etc.) while holding all other variables constant. In other words, we are interested in the effect that an independent variable has on the outcome of interest. To test our juggernaut theory of state repression, we use three binary dependent variables (onset, termination, and recurrence) and one ordered dependent variable (escalation). For the binary dependent variables, we employ discrete time duration models—specifically probit regression and for the ordered dependent variable we use a related ordered probit estimator.[45] Consistent with standard practice, we include a linear counter of time to account for duration dependence in the models with the binary dependent variables, and use robust standard errors clustered on the country/spell to deal with serial correlation.[46]

In order to ensure the validity and robustness of the results, it is worth mentioning that while regression models provide powerful ways to test theories, they also make important assumptions that must be accounted for. For the present analysis, we are most concerned with issues related to omitted variable bias or the ignorability assumption. Briefly, this implies that the independent variables of interest (e.g., democratization) are randomly

---

[45] This estimation technique is largely equivalent with the government repression literature that uses logistic regression models (Simmons 2009; Davenport 2007).

[46] Model fit statistics such as the AUC indicate that a linear counter of time is a better fit for the data compared to a squared or cubic polynomial of time.

assigned between treated and control units conditional on the inclusion of confounders (i.e., variables) in the model. While this is possible, it is often difficult to control for all factors that differ between treated and control groups in observational studies such as the current one because only some potential confounders are observable. Put simply, our models may suffer from omitted variable bias in that there are some unobserved variables that affect both the independent variable(s) and the error term (and consequently the dependent variable) in the models. Failure to meet this assumption results in the model being unidentified which in turn can produce biased results.

We mention the position taken above because the potential problem with the present analysis is that governments (or governments in spells) may systematically differ from another in ways that cannot be controlled for using observed data. For example, it is possible that some governments may be predisposed to initiate LSSR due to political culture, institutional arrangements, organization of government security forces, etc., and we cannot control for these factors due to data limitations. The inability to include these measures in models potentially produces biased results. It is therefore essential that scholars account for this important threat to inference.

To account for this potential problem, in the appendices at the conclusion of this book, we employ two different strategies: (1) fixed effects regression and (2) instrumental variable (IV) regression. As we report, the fixed effects and IV regression results are consistent with those in the main text and thus we maintain confidence in the findings reported in the chapters that follow.

Appendices

2.A Descriptive Statistics

Table 2.1 Descriptive Statistics

Onset Model	N	Min	Max	Mean
Democracy	2,666	0	1	0.56
Democratization	2,666	0	1	0.04
Civil Resistance (Domestic)	2,666	0	1	0.002
Civil Resistance (International)	2,666	0	1	0.02
INGO Presence	2,666	0	1	0.43
Judicial Aspects of Democracy	2,666	0	1	0.78
Human Rights Treaties	2,666	0	3	1.5

Onset Model	N	Min	Max	Mean
IGO Membership	2,666	1	129	56
Sanctions	2,666	0	1	0.05
Neutral Interventions	2,666	0	1	0.04
Pro-government Interventions	2,666	0	1	0.07
Anti-government Interventions	2,666	0	1	0.04
Civil Conflict	2,666	0	1	0.04
Economic Development	2,666	503	8583	46,065
Population	2,666	11	20	15
Youth Bulge	2,666	12.9	41.1	26
Civil War Termination	2,666	0	1	0.006

Escalation/Termination Models	N	Min	Max	Mean
Democracy	2,539	0	1	0.28
Democratization	2,539	0	1	0.08
Civil Resistance (Domestic)	2,539	0	1	0.02
Civil Resistance (International)	2,539	0	1	0.03
INGO Presence	2,539	0	1	0.35
Judicial Aspects of Democracy	2,539	0	1	0.46
Human Rights Treaties	2,539	0	3	1.6
IGO Membership	2,539	1	108	54
Sanctions	2,539	0	1	0.15
Neutral Interventions	2,539	0	1	0.12
Pro-government Interventions	2,539	0	1	0.11
Anti-government Interventions	2,539	0	1	0.13
Civil Conflict	2,539	0	1	0.32
Economic Development	2,539	276	31,049	3,823
Population	2,539	11	20	16
Youth Bulge	2,539	15	43	32
Civil War Termination	2,539	0	1	0.04

Recurrence Model	N	Min	Max	Mean
Democracy	1,015	0	1	0.44
Democratization	1,015	0	1	0.11
Civil Resistance (Domestic)	1,015	0	1	0.003
Civil Resistance (International)	1,015	0	1	0.02
INGO Presence	1,015	0	1	0.36
Judicial Aspects of Democracy	1,015	0	1	0.71
Human Rights Treaties	1,015	0	3	1.78
IGO Membership	1,015	2	109	56
Sanctions	1,015	0	1	0.05
Neutral Interventions	1,015	0	1	0.04
Pro-government Interventions	1,015	0	1	0.04
Anti-government Interventions	1,015	0	1	0.06
Civil Conflict	1,015	0	1	0.05
Economic Development	1,015	503	32,307	5916
Population	1,015	11	18	15
Youth Bulge	1,015	12	41	29
Civil War Termination	1,015	0	1	0.01

2.B List of LSSR Spells

Table 2.2 LSSR Spells, 1976–2006

Country	Start Year	End Year
Albania	1976	2006
Algeria	1979	1979
Algeria	1988	ongoing
Angola	1976	ongoing
Argentina	1976	1983
Argentina	1989	1991
Argentina	1996	2002
Argentina	2004	2006
Armenia	2002	2002
Armenia	2007	ongoing
Azerbaijan	1992	1994
Azerbaijan	2004	ongoing
Bahrain	1976	1996
Bangladesh	1976	ongoing
Belarus	1997	2002
Belarus	2004	ongoing
Benin	1980	1981
Benin	1985	1989
Benin	2005	ongoing
Bhutan	1991	1997
Bolivia	1976	1992
Bolivia	1999	2006
Bosnia and Herzegovina	1992	2000
Brazil	1976	ongoing
Bulgaria	1976	1989
Bulgaria	1999	2001
Bulgaria	2005	ongoing
Burkina Faso	1983	1983
Burkina Faso	1988	1988
Burkina Faso	1994	1995
Burkina Faso	1999	2002
Burkina Faso	2006	ongoing
Burundi	1985	ongoing
Cambodia	1976	ongoing
Cameroon	1976	1978
Cameroon	1984	1985
Cameroon	1991	ongoing
Central African Republic	1978	1985
Central African Republic	2001	ongoing
Chad	1977	ongoing
Chile	1976	1993
China	1976	ongoing
Colombia	1977	ongoing

Comoros	1976	1978
Comoros	1985	1987
Comoros	1992	1993
Comoros	1999	1999
Comoros	2007	ongoing
Congo	1987	1987
Congo	1993	ongoing
Croatia	1992	1999
Cuba	1976	2001
Cuba	2004	ongoing
Czech Republic	1976	1989
Democratic Republic of the Congo	1977	ongoing
Djibouti	1991	1994
Djibouti	1998	2001
Djibouti	2006	ongoing
Dominican Republic	1976	1980
Dominican Republic	1984	1988
Dominican Republic	1996	ongoing
Ecuador	1977	1978
Ecuador	1985	ongoing
Egypt	1976	ongoing
El Salvador	1976	ongoing
Equatorial Guinea	1976	1978
Equatorial Guinea	1990	2002
Equatorial Guinea	2004	ongoing
Eritrea	1997	ongoing
Ethiopia	1976	ongoing
Fiji	1987	1987
Fiji	2000	2001
Gabon	1981	1981
Gabon	1988	1988
Gabon	1994	1994
Gabon	2005	ongoing
Gambia	1981	1981
Gambia	2000	2000
Gambia	2006	ongoing
Georgia	1992	ongoing
Ghana	1976	1976
Ghana	1977	1986
Ghana	1991	1994
Ghana	2002	2002
Ghana	2004	ongoing
Greece	1986	1986
Greece	1994	1996
Greece	2006	2006
Grenada	1980	1983
Guatemala	1976	ongoing
Guinea	1976	2001
Guinea	2004	ongoing
Guinea-Bissau	1996	1999
Guinea-Bissau	2005	2005
Guyana	1980	1984
Guyana	2000	2006

Continued

Table 2.2 *Continued*

Country	Start Year	End Year
Haiti	1976	ongoing
Honduras	1980	ongoing
Hungary	1976	1976 .
India	1976	ongoing
Indonesia	1976	ongoing
Iran	1976	ongoing
Iraq	1976	ongoing
Israel	1976	1978
Israel	1984	ongoing
Italy	1988	1988
Ivory Coast (Cote d'Ivoire)	1992	1992
Ivory Coast (Cote d'Ivoire)	1996	1996
Ivory Coast (Cote d'Ivoire)	2000	ongoing
Jamaica	1988	1988
Jamaica	1992	ongoing
Jordan	1978	2002
Jordan	2006	ongoing
Kazakhstan	2000	2002
Kazakhstan	2004	ongoing
Kenya	1978	1978
Kenya	1982	ongoing
Kuwait	1983	1985
Kuwait	1990	1995
Kyrgyz Republic	1999	1999
Kyrgyz Republic	2004	ongoing
Laos	1976	1988
Laos	1998	ongoing
Lebanon	1989	ongoing
Lesotho	1979	1994
Lesotho	1998	1998
Lesotho	2007	ongoing
Liberia	1979	ongoing
Libya	1976	ongoing
Macedonia	1997	2002
Madagascar	1976	1976
Madagascar	1988	1993
Madagascar	2002	2002
Malawi	1976	1976
Malawi	1983	1992
Malawi	2002	ongoing
Malaysia	1976	1985
Malaysia	1991	1991
Malaysia	1995	1998
Malaysia	2002	2002
Mali	1977	1984
Mali	1990	1995
Mauritania	1978	1984
Mauritania	1988	1992

Mauritania	2000	2002
Mauritania	2004	ongoing
Mexico	1976	ongoing
Moldova	1992	1993
Moldova	1999	1999
Moldova	2003	2004
Morocco	1976	1996
Morocco	2003	ongoing
Mozambique	1976	2001
Mozambique	2004	ongoing
Myanmar	1976	ongoing
Namibia	1998	2002
Nepal	1976	ongoing
Nicaragua	1976	2006
Niger	1979	1984
Niger	1990	1999
Niger	2007	ongoing
Nigeria	1978	1978
Nigeria	1984	ongoing
North Korea (Democratic People's Republic of Korea)	1997	ongoing
North Yemen	1985	1985
North Yemen	1979	1990
Pakistan	1977	ongoing
Panama	1987	1991
Panama	1996	1996
Papua New Guinea	1988	1996
Papua New Guinea	2003	ongoing
Paraguay	1976	1990
Paraguay	1994	ongoing
Peru	1976	2006
Philippines	1976	ongoing
Poland	1976	1987
Romania	1976	2000
Romania	2005	ongoing
Russia	1990	ongoing
Rwanda	1982	1982
Rwanda	1986	1986
Rwanda	1990	ongoing
Saudi Arabia	1976	1976
Saudi Arabia	1980	ongoing
Senegal	1985	2003
Senegal	2006	ongoing
Sierra Leone	1976	1977
Sierra Leone	1983	1983
Sierra Leone	1991	ongoing
Singapore	1976	1982
Solomon Islands	1999	2003
Somalia	1977	ongoing
South Africa	1976	ongoing
South Korea (Republic of Korea)	1980	1996
South Korea (Republic of Korea)	2002	2002

Continued

Table 2.2 *Continued*

Country	Start Year	End Year
Spain	1976	1976
Spain	1980	1980
Spain	2002	2002
Sri Lanka	1976	ongoing
Sudan	1976	ongoing
Suriname	1981	1990
Swaziland	1993	1994
Swaziland	2006	ongoing
Syria	1976	ongoing
Tajikistan	1992	1999
Tajikistan	2004	ongoing
Tanzania	1976	1978
Tanzania	1983	1983
Tanzania	1995	ongoing
Thailand	1976	1986
Thailand	1990	1994
Thailand	1998	ongoing
Togo	1976	1978
Togo	1983	1984
Togo	1990	1994
Togo	1998	ongoing
Trinidad and Tobago	2005	2005
Tunisia	1977	ongoing
Turkey	1976	ongoing
Turkmenistan	2003	ongoing
Uganda	1976	ongoing
Ukraine	1999	ongoing
United Arab Emirates	2002	2002
United Kingdom	2005	2005
United States	2004	ongoing
Uruguay	1976	1984
Uruguay	1990	1990
USSR	1976	1987
Uzbekistan	2001	ongoing
Venezuela	1978	ongoing
Vietnam (Socialist Republic of Vietnam)	1976	1991
Vietnam (Socialist Republic of Vietnam)	2004	ongoing
Yugoslavia	1976	ongoing
Zambia	1976	1993
Zambia	1997	ongoing
Zimbabwe	1980	1987
Zimbabwe	1998	ongoing

2.C LSSR Examples

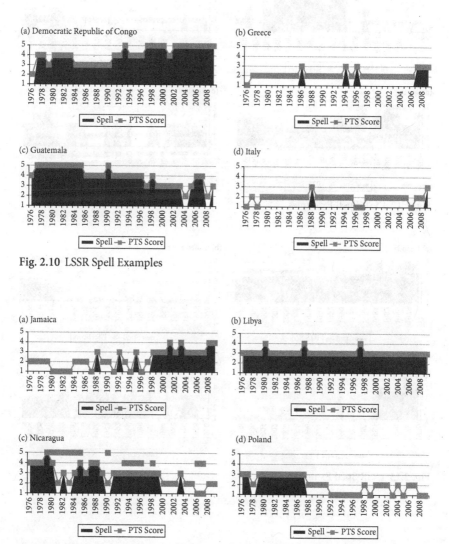

Fig. 2.10 LSSR Spell Examples

Fig. 2.11 LSSR Spell Examples

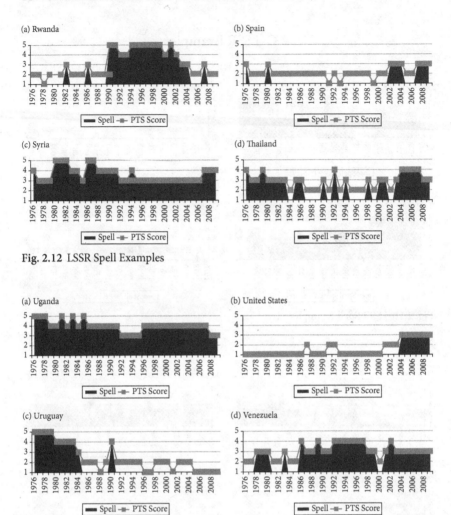

Fig. 2.12 LSSR Spell Examples

Fig. 2.13 LSSR Spell Examples

3

Starting Spells

3.1 Introduction

We begin our investigation regarding the life cycle of large-scale state repression by considering how they start (i.e., onset). As discussed above, we use logistic regression to test our theoretical argument because our dependent variable is a binary measure. Here, the dependent variable equals 1 when a LSSR starts, and zero otherwise.[47] Despite the new dependent variable of LSSR initiation in the literature of repression/human rights violation, the estimation approach is actually quite standard within the literature on government repression in particular and social science more generally.[48] Four models are estimated.

Within the first analysis, we discuss the baseline model with the leading control variables from the literature, including population, economic development, youth bulges, ongoing civil war, and civil war termination. In the second analysis, we include the control variables above plus the domestic factors including domestic-international hybrids: democracy, democratization, civil resistance movements, internationally backed civil resistance movements, and INGO presence. In the third analysis, we present the leading control variables plus measures that account for international as well as domestic-international hybrids such as international human rights treaties, preferential trade agreements (PTAs), IGO membership, economic sanctions, and military interventions (pro-government, anti-government, and neutral interventions). Finally, we present the full model (the fourth analysis) with the controls as well as diverse domestic and international

---

[47] The data that we use in this analysis are what are called "left-censored" in that several spells were ongoing prior to 1976, the year we start our analysis. While this is not ideal, it is due to the PTS data which only goes back to 1976. To account for this, we estimate a robustness check in which we include a control variable in the model that accounts for spells that started prior to 1976. The binary measure equals 1 for all spells that began before 1976 and zero otherwise. The key results are robust to the inclusion of this variable, and available upon request.

[48] We also include a counter of time within our models in order to account for duration dependence and cluster our standard errors on the country to help deal with serial correlation.

The Death and Life of State Repression: Understanding Onset, Escalation, Termination, and Recurrence.
Christian Davenport and Benjamin J. Appel, Oxford University Press. © Oxford University Press 2022.
DOI: 10.1093/oso/9780197655375.003.0004

variables. To facilitate clear exposition, we present the results using coefficient plots that include the coefficient estimate and 95 percent confidence intervals.[49] Acknowledging that statistical findings are not always clearly comprehensible within tables or figures, we also present post-estimation predicted probabilities after the results to assess the substantive effects of the statistically significant variables.

3.2 Results for Control Variables

Earlier, we noted that our research could potentially be quite different from the last few decades of research on repressive variation because of the focus on a new unit of analysis and new dependent variables. From the results, however, we discover that some of our onset findings are similar to those that have been identified previously whereas other findings are not.

Recall, that we maintained an LSSR would be initiated when diverse threats were present as this provided the core identity and purpose around which the cohort in favor of repression would cohere. This is broadly what we see across the models estimated. For example, results disclose that governments are more likely to start large-scale, severe repression spells when they are faced with ongoing civil conflict and when countries are more populous. These both represent distinct forms of threats—one explicitly behavioral in nature while the other is more demographic. Across models, we also consistently see that governments with higher levels of economic development are less inclined to engage in LSSRs. As conceived, this economic measure provides an alternative mechanism of influence for those in government and consistently it reduces the necessity for large-scale, severe repression.

In contrast to our expectations as well as prior results within the variation literature of repressive action, the youth bulge measure fails to meet statistical significance in three models, and is only weakly significant in the baseline model before other variables are included. Additionally, we see that the time counter fails to reach standard levels of significance. These results are interesting and somewhat puzzling because some of the more sophisticated

---

[49] A variable is statistically significant at the two-tailed, .05 level if the confidence intervals do not cross zero. Given debates about level of significance (i.e., .05 vs. .10), we consider a variable to be "borderline" significant when it is significant at the .10 level.

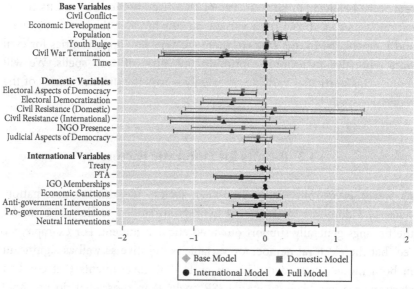

Fig. 3.1 Determinants of LSSR Onset, 1976–2006

analyses on the subject found that youth bulges were a key predictor of repression when considered with a repressive measure that moves upward or downward across a wide range of values (e.g., Hill and Jones (2014) and Nordås and Davenport (2013)). To be clear, the insignificant findings here do not suggest that youth bulges are unrelated to all aspects of government repression considered here. Rather, it suggests that youth bulges are not important for the onset phase of the repression life cycle. This is something that we will discuss further below because this variable is important for other phases.

Further differentiating our research from prior research, we find that although civil war termination is negative and thus in the expected direction, it fails to reach statistical significance. This result is not unexpected, as most governments engulfed in civil war are believed to already be in repressive spells (which is not actually true). The finding does prove to be intriguing however for it reveals the somewhat neglected complexity of government repression with civil war (Hill, Jr. 2016). For example, some work identifies that LSSR is one of the reasons why civil wars occur in the first place (Davenport, Armstrong, and Lichbach 2006; Young 2013). Some research also identifies that civil war itself further ramps up and institutionalizes repressive behavior to such an extent that it continues beyond its termination (Gates et al. 2010)—a variant on our broader theme of stickiness and juggernauts. In this context, there are very few opportunities for civil wars repressive to terminate prior to the onset of such spells. We will discuss this particular variable repeatedly across the distinct phases of the repressive spell.

3.3 Results for Domestic Factors

As we observe from Figure 2.1, when factors identified within nation-states and domestic-international hybrids are added to the basic model, the findings generally support our theoretical argument. For example, we see that the electoral democracy variable is negative as well as significant in both models estimated. This suggests that governments that conduct elections are less likely to start LSSR spells than those that do not hold them. This work is directly in ' line with the expectations of existing government repression literature; indeed, it is consistent with what has previously been identified as one of (if not) the most stable, statistically and substantively important findings in the literature—the "domestic democratic peace".

Other aspects of democracy appear relevant for LSSR onset furthering the point. For instance, we see similar results for the electoral democratization variable as governments that recently underwent a transition (opening electorally) are less likely to initiate an LSSR spell compared to governments that have not opened up. Although much less frequently examined than the level of democracy, this finding is generally consistent with the domestic democratic peace. Related, we see that the judicial democracy variable is negative in its impact, although it misses statistical significance at conventional levels. Taken together, the results give strong support to the role of democratic institutions in preventing LSSR spells.

Interesting results are found with regard to the civil resistance and NGO variables. Specifically, we find that domestic-only civil resistance movements fail to come close to statistical significance in both models. This suggests that there is no systematic relationship between these types of movements and the prevention of LSSR spells. In contrast, civil resistance movements that receive international support are negative and statistically significant in the estimated model, although they are only borderline significant in the full model. While the findings are relatively weak (from a statistical point of view), they nonetheless suggest that particular nonviolent movements may be effective at inhibiting large-scale, severe repression spells.[50]

Similar to civil resistance, the NGO variable is negative in its impact but, different from the civil resistance measure, it misses statistical significance across both models. Here, we conclude that NGO activity has little systematic impact on decreasing the possibility of an LSSR getting started.[51]

3.4 Results for International Factors

In Figure 2.1, we show the results from our empirical investigation when international variables are introduced. Deviating from popular expectations but not our theoretical argument, overall we see very little support for international factors playing a role in the onset of LSSR. We do observe, however, that one variable: the Preferential Trade Agreement (PTA) measure is negative and statistically significant across estimated models. This suggests that governments with at least one PTA are less likely to initiate LSSR spells. Such a finding is largely consistent with the extant literature which finds a similar correlation between PTAs and human rights practices (but see Spilker and Böhmelt (2013)).

In contrast, we find no support for international law and the related IGO membership variables. This may seem somewhat surprising to readers in that it suggests that international law does not prevent governments from engaging in the worst forms of repressive behavior which is a consistent claim made by some of the more prominent pieces on human rights. At the same time, this is not enitrely unexpected because recent research suggests that the influence of international law is conditional on other factors, such as domestic rule of law systems and regime-type—suggesting a different domestic-international hybrid (Lupu 2013b; Simmons 2009).

[50] Now some may be concerned that repressive behavior might hinder civil resistance movements thereby hindering the ability to impact state coercive and forceful behavior but this gives far too much credit to repression. Indeed, researchers of civil resistance note that repressive action does not impact the probability of successful mobilization (Chenoweth, Perkoski, and Kang 2017). This mirrors the broader finding within the literature that repression has inconsistent impacts on challenging behavior (Davenport 2007).
[51] We also estimated the impact of domestic-only NGOs on LSSR spell onset. The variable is not significant. We exclude it from the primary analysis because the measure suffers from missing data problems, and we lose too many observations in the model when we include it.

From our empirical investigation, we also see little support for what are generally characterized as "stick" variables. For example, pro-government and anti-government military interventions as well as economic sanctions fail to reach standard levels of statistical significance in established models. Government efforts at LSSR are thus not hindered by external efforts that are believed to prevent such behavior. Neutral interventions are significant and positive in their effects on LSSR onset, which actually suggests that this type of intervention is associated with a higher probability of LSSR spells beginning. This along with the findings for the biased/non-neutral interventions raise some red flags about the utility of interventions as a mechanism of preventing LSSR. Indeed, results push us to conclude that these policies directly exacerbate situations of large-scale human rights violation, making their initiation more (and not less) likely.

3.4.1 Substantive Effects

Above we identified which variables were significant in their effects on LSSR onset. In this section, we address how much of an impact they wield. To do this, we present the post-estimation effects. Specifically, we show the predicted probability that a government initiates a repressive spell at different values of the statistically significant explanatory variable. For binary variables, we present the predicated probability at "0" to "1" and we present it across the range of values for interval-level or continuous variables (i.e., 20th to 80th percentile). Following the advice of Hanmer and Ozan Kalkan (2013), we hold all other variables at their observed values.[52] Within subsequent chapters we merge this discussion with statistical significance but we keep them separate here in order to facilitate the clear understanding of the procedure that we will follow.

To begin, we consider the impact of the variables that were used within the basic model (i.e., the standard set of controls included in a study of state repression). In Figure 3.2a, we present the results for the impact of civil war on the probability of LSSR onset. As expected, this variable has a strong influence. In the absence of civil war, the probability that a government initiates a spell is 9 percent but this probability is increased to 20 percent

---

[52] In some cases, the 95 percent confidence intervals overlap. This does not indicate that the variable is not statistically significant (Austin and Hux 2002).

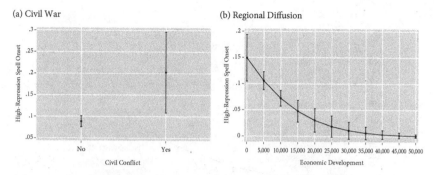

Fig. 3.2 Predicted Probabilities for LSSR Onset, Control Variables

when civil wars are underway. Substantively, therefore, this form of political conflict increases the probability of sustained, large-scale repression by about 150 percent! While this impact is substantial, it should be noted that there is still some variation unaccounted for. Many believe that repressive behavior is largely (if not) completely driven by civil war with the former being derivative of the latter. Our results indicate that this is simply not the case. Indeed, there is a significant amount of LSSR examined outside of civil war.

From our analyses, population appears to have a large impact on onset. Specifically, we find that the probability that a government initiates a spell increases from about 3 percent at the lowest levels of population to 30 percent at the highest levels. Governments with large populations and the corresponding socio-political control problems that these involve tend to see an increased the likelihood that an LSSR would be initiated.

In line with the previous literature, we see that economic development has a strong impact on reducing the probability of spell onset. Here, it is revealed that the poorest governments have a 15 percent chance of spell onset but this falls to almost zero percent for the richest governments, which provides them with diverse options for socio-political control. It is thus clear that economic development is a very important factor when it comes to preventing large-scale, severe repression.

Regarding our domestically oriented variables beyond the basic model, several were revealed to be statistically important and our discussion here also reveals that many are substantively important as well. For example, the impact of democracy is most directly relevant to our theoretical argument. Results disclose that a nondemocratic government initiates an LSSR spell at 12 percent but this probability declines to only 6 percent for democratic governments. This suggests that democracies are 50 percent less likely to

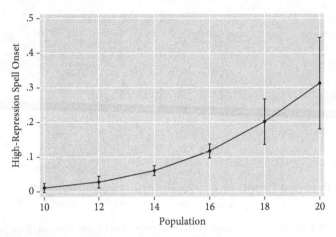

Fig. 3.3 Population, Control Variable

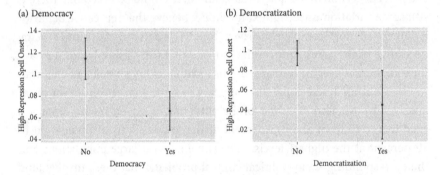

Fig. 3.4 Predicted Probabilities for LSSR Onset, Domestic Variables

engage in an large-scale, severe repression. The domestic democratic peace and the costs associated with these forms of government work in reducing the likelihood of LSSR spells directly in line with the research concerned with repressive variation. Related to this, we see that the probability of an autocratic regime initiating a spell of LSSR is again close to 12 percent but this decreases to about 5 percent in governments that recently underwent a democratic transition. Democratization thus decreases the probability that a regime starts an LSSR spell by almost 60 percent!

Lastly, the substantive results for the internationally oriented variables are quite informative. Specifically, we find that governments without Preferential Trade Agreements have about a 10 percent probability of initiating LSSR, but this drops to about 6 percent when they sign at least one PTA. This suggests that these agreements decrease the probability of LSSR by

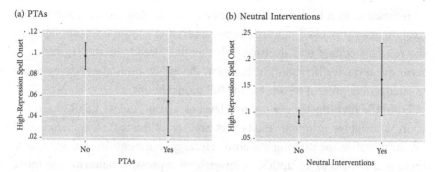

Fig. 3.5 Predicted Probabilities for LSSR Spell Onset, International Variables

about 40 percent. In contrast to our expectations and those of others, we find that neutral interventions are actually associated with a higher probability of spell onset. In particular, we see the probability that a government starts an LSSR spell in the absence of a neutral intervention is 9 percent, but this increases to 16 percent in the presence of a neutral intervention. This means that neutral interventions increase the probability of spell onset by about 77 percent, once again raising questions about the efficacy of these types of interventions when viewed in a preventive capacity.

3.5   Onset of LSSR Models, Version 2

Within this section, we continue to focus on the onset of LSSR spells, but we restrict our analysis to countries that have already experienced a small increase in repression (i.e., moving from 1 to 2 on the PTS scale) prior to the onset of sustained, large-scale violent activity.[53] Such an investigation is important because it allows us to check the robustness of the results using a slightly different set of cases (those which have undergone a minor escalation in repressive behavior), while also allowing us to determine if some domestic or international factors only have an impact on LSSR onset once a government already engages in some repression. The reason for adopting this approach emerges from our theoretical argument regarding the potential difficulties presented by a repressive process that is gathering momentum from one that essentially jumps from some lower level

---

[53] We integrate the discussion of the substantive effects with the regression results to streamline the discussion of this section.

of repression to a higher level. As conceived, the former should be more easily/readily provoked upwards because (even at a lower-level application) the relevant cohort and decision calculus has already started to move in favor of repressive behavior. In contrast, the latter should be less amenable to change. We present results for the full model below.

From the investigation of pre-low level escalation before LSSR onset, the control variables produce results that are very similar to the main set of results as well as the existing literature. Here, governments in civil war where there had been a prior uptick in lower-level repressive behavior are more likely to start an LSSR spell. In particular, the predicted probability that a government initiates a repressive spell in the absence of civil war was about 9 percent but this moves to 21 percent when the government had previously moved from the lowest level of repression to the next highest and a civil war took place. We (again) see that governments are more likely to initiate large-scale repression when they have larger populations, as the predicted probability increases from 4 to 18 percent when we go from low population to high levels of it. Now, this does not mean that there are changes in the size of the population, which would be a very different dynamic. Rather, this means that nation-states with large populations where there has also been a

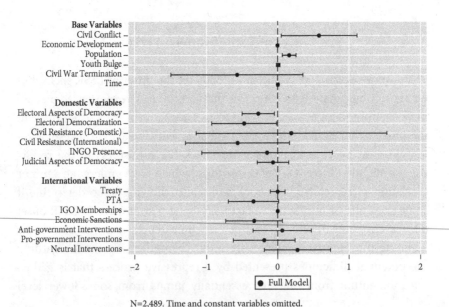

N=2,489. Time and constant variables omitted.
Robust standard errors, clustered on country.

Fig. 3.6 Determinants of LSSR Onset, Low-Level Repression, 1976–2006

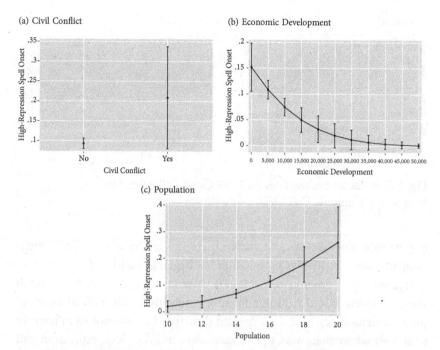

Fig. 3.7 Predicted Probabilities for LSSR Onset Following Low-Level Repression, Control Variables

low-level increase in repressive behavior act quite different from those with smaller ones—all else equal. Once more, we see that governments are less likely to start an LSSR spell when they are from richer governments, as shown by the positive and statistically significant results for the economic development variable. Poorer governments have about an 11 percent probability of escalating to an LSSR spell but this decreases to near zero for wealthier states. Mirroring earlier research, the civil war termination and youth bulge variables fail to reach standard levels of significance.

Regarding domestic variables, we again see that both democracy and democratization are negative and statistically significant in their effects on LSSR onset. The probability that a nondemocratic regime which had previously moved from the lowest level of repression to the next highest initiates an LSSR spell is 11 percent but this decreases to 7 percent for a democracy. Likewise, after moving from the lowest level of government repression to the next level, a recently democratized regime decreases the probability of spell onset from about 11 to 4 percent compared to an autocratic regime. Both the statistical significance and the substantive results lend further support to the

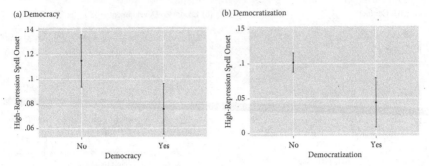

Fig. 3.8 Predicted Probabilities for LSSR Onset Following Low-Level Repression, Domestic Variables

importance of democratic institutions in preventing the onset of LSSR spells even after some repressive momentum has began to build.

Interestingly, numerous variables are close to an impact but do not reach standard levels of statistical significance. For example, the judicial aspect of political democracy is in the expected direction but it is not significant in situations where there was a prior escalation in lower-level repression and a move to LSSR is made. We see similar results for the variables associated with some civil resistance movements. Purely domestic movements fail to have an impact on the onset of LSSR spells, but the variable on civil resistance movements with international support is negative as expected but just misses statistical significance. Finally, the INGO participation variable is negative as expected but it also fails to reach standard levels of significance.

Considering international variables, the results (once more) reveal that at the onset stage there is a limited role played by these factors. For example, after moving repression from the lowest level to the next highest but still outside of a spell, the PTA variable is negative and statistically significant although only borderline significant. This suggests that governments which have increased repression from the lower levels and that are economically integrated into the international community are less inclined to initiate LSSR spells. The probability that a regime with no PTAs initiates a spell is 10 percent but this decreases to about 6 percent when the government has at least one PTA. In contrast, we see that after moving from the lowest level to the next highest (but still not within a spell) economic sanctions are negative and borderline statistically significant (i.e., only significant at .10, two-tailed level). This indicates that economic sanctions have a chance at preventing low-repressive governments from escalating to higher-level repression if

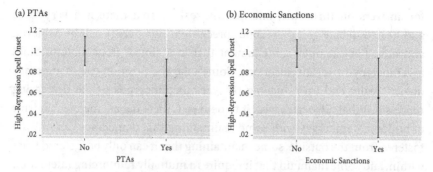

Fig. 3.9 Predicted Probabilities for LSSR Spell Onset Following Low-Level Repression, International Variables

action is taken at the lowest levels of repressive mobilization. Specifically, governments with economic sanctions have about a 10 percent probability of starting an LSSR spell but this falls to 5 percent when the international community has enacted sanctions against the regime in question. While we caution that this finding is only weakly significant, it nonetheless suggests that, at least in some situations, the international community might be able to impose some costs on governments that prevent them from repressing further.

After moving from the lowest level to the next highest but still not within a spell, both IGO membership and the treaty variables fail to reach standard levels of significance. Finally, all three military intervention variables fail to reach standard levels of significance. This again raises doubts about the utility of these foreign policy tools to prevent high-levels of repression.

3.6 The Determinants of Electoral Democratization

The previous two analyses indicate that democratic electoral institutions are some of the key barriers to the initiation of an LSSR spell. In particular, results disclose that both established and new democracies are less likely to engage in these forms of repression compared to autocratic governments! While important and providing an important clue into how LSSRs start, we recognize that democratic consolidation and democratization are very difficult to achieve in their own right and thus knowledge of their pacifying influence should only be met with partial satisfaction. It would be nice to know why these changes take place. When considering the literature for answers on this topic, one quickly realizes that there is a very large and heated debate going on about precisely if democracy can be achieved and how. For example, some lament that it is almost impossible to build a democracy in certain locations. Some take the position that democracy doesn't really end up achieving the various policy goals (like decreasing repression) that advocates wish it to deliver. Others debate the mechanisms of building democracy with some maintaining that democracy can only be fostered from the outside, some maintaining that it can only be fostered from within, and some maintain that it requires a mutually reinforcing interaction between the two influences. Given this situation, it seems useful for us to help provide more guidance about both the direct and indirect factors associated with LSSR spell onset. Toward this end, we examine what drives electorally oriented democratic transition.

To facilitate this investigation, we select electoral aspects of democracy because it was the more robustly influential aspect of democracy identified above and this feature of democratic government has been an interest for political theorists, social activists, and policymakers alike—for decades. In many respects, it is the cornerstone around which many discussions about political progress are built. Finally, it is useful to engage in this analysis as a way to better contextualize discussion about electoral violence which (because of its focus on elections) generally tends to play down or completely ignore broader patterns in government repression. Indeed, with the focus on these types of events, researchers tend to miss the longer-term as well as larger-scale behavior undertaken by political authorities which gives the idea of the spell a particular significance.

Drawing on extant research, we use probit to estimate our models in which we present the results for the sample estimated on autocratic governments (Przeworski et al. 2000; Boix 2003). This allows us to calculate the likelihood that a government that started the year as autocratic transitioned to democracy by the end of the year.[54] Specifically, we create a new dependent variable—democratic transitions—that equals "1" if the government in question recently democratized and zero otherwise. We then regress this variable

---

[54] We recognize that some democratization scholars examine all types of regimes and focus on both democratic transitions and democratic consolidation. We restrict our sample to autocratic states due to our interest in democratic transitions only.

on the same set of measures from the previous analyses on a global sample of nondemocratic governments from 1976 to 2006.[55]

Below, results are presented for the full model from the LSSR onset analysis below plus two additional variables that previous scholarship has found to be related to democratization: (1) past transitions in the government in question and (2) regional diffusion of democratization (Gassebner, Lamla, and Vreeland 2013; Ulfelder 2010). Concerning the new variables, the democratic diffusion variable is measured as the proportion of neighboring states that have democratized in the previous two years using the Cheibub, Gandhi, and Vreeland measure (2010). Scholars put forward different reasons to explain this relationship. There is the demonstration effect where actors learn from and emulate neighboring countries that have undergone successful transitions (Gleditsch 2009). Scholars also suggest that neighboring democracies provide more resources to democratic movements, while others argue the costs of ruling for autocrats increase as democracy becomes more common among neighbors (Celestino and Gleditsch 2013). Concerning the latter variable, we also add the number of previous democratic transitions in the country to the model again using the Cheibub, Gandhi, and Vreeland (2010) measure. Similar to the demonstration effect, domestic actors will be more confident that they can successfully democratize when the state has a history of doing so, leading domestic actors to be more likely to push for such transitions in the next period (Gassebner, Lamla, and Vreeland 2013).

The results from the democratization model are useful to observe. For example, we see that economic development decreases the likelihood of democratization. This result is important because it contributes to an important debate about the role of development in democratization. Dating back to Lipset's (1959) groundbreaking work on modernization theory, several scholars found that economic development increases the likelihood of democratic transitions. At the same time, other, more recent work called this link into question, such as Przeworski's (1991) comprehensive work on the correlates of democratization. Likewise, Gassebner, Lamla, and Vreeland (2013) who evaluate over 1.7 million regressions using extreme bounds analysis to identify the most robust measures of democratization find that economic development has a robust negative effect on the probability of a

---

[55] In addition, as a robustness check, we create a second variable that equals 1 if the state in question democratized in the past year and zero otherwise. The results are robust to this alternative coding rule.

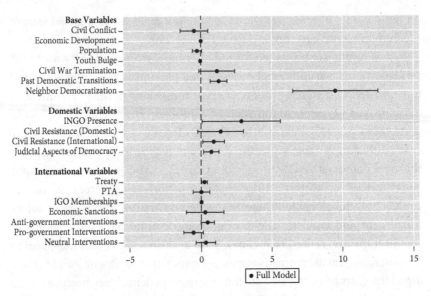

N=1,361. Time and constant variables omitted.
Robust standard errors, clustered on country.

Fig. 3.10 The Determinants of Electoral Democratization, 1976–2006

democratic transition. While there is still an important debate, our research provides some support for the negative link between economic development and democratization.

From the results, population is negative and statistically significant in its impact. This suggests that more populous countries are less likely to democratize in a given year, which is interesting given that scholars disagree on this relationship (Gassebner, Lamla, and Vreeland 2013; Acemoglu et al. 2008).

As expected, we see that ongoing civil war is negative in its impact but it fails to reach significance, while civil war termination is positive in its impact but is only borderline significant. The youth bulge variable also fails to reach statistical significance, although it is negative in terms of effect. These results are not unexpected given that scholars generally fail to find a robust relationship between them and democratic transitions.

Overall, we find strong support for both the diffusion variable and the number of past transitions. These findings are consistent with several recent articles on democratization (Gleditsch and Ward 2006; Gleditsch 2009; Celestino and Gleditsch 2013; Gassebner, Lamla, and Vreeland 2013).

When considered, the domestic-based variables produce interesting results. For example, we see that judicial aspects of political democracy are positive and significant in their impact on electoral democracy, which is consistent with the work of Gibler and Randazzo (2011). This research suggests that governments with more independent judiciaries are more likely to undergo electoral democratic transitions, and, furthermore, provide an indirect link to the prevention of LSSR onset. The finding further suggests that democratization scholars should further examine the link between judicial aspects of democracy and electoral ones given that we find strong support for it and there appear to be few studies on it.

We see that domestically generated civil resistance movements are positive but are only borderline significant. In contrast, the findings indicate that democratization is more likely in the presence of internationally backed resistance movements, where this variable is positive and statistically significant. Given these results are similar to several other studies that find a relationship between nonviolent movements and democratization-except the part about external support which has not really received that much attention, it seems useful to explore these relationships further (Bratton and Van de Walle 1997; Celestino and Gleditsch 2013; Chenoweth, Stephan, and Stephan 2011; Ulfelder 2005). Along with our juggernaut argument, scholars suggest that civil resistance is successful because it leads to mass participation, destabilizing as well as undermining autocratic rulers and ultimately causing them to make concessions/movements towards democracy to offset the increased pressure on them (Celestino and Gleditsch 2013; Chenoweth, Stephan, and Stephan 2011). At the same time, the distinction we make between domestic-only civil resistance movements and internationally backed ones advances this literature which largely overlooks the role of external support in influencing the outcomes of nonviolent movements. The findings in our analyses provide evidence in favor of the relationship between nonviolence and democratization, with the new contribution/nuance about externally supported domestic movements.

In contrast to the LSSR models, INGO membership is positive and statistically significant in its effect on democratization. This indicates that when a government interacts with more INGOs, it is more likely to democratize. This again suggests the vital link between domestic groups and international actors for both democratization and LSSR as well as further illuminates the causal chain involved.

Also in contrast to the results above, we see mixed results for the international-based variables. Interestingly, these findings suggest that governments that ratify human rights treaties are more likely to democratize compared to governments that refrain from doing so. Similar to the above, it is possible that treaty ratification spurs domestic mobilization which leads to democratic transitions (Simmons 2009). Finally, we find some support for the link between IGO membership and LSSR onset. While this is not a robust finding, it is in line with work by Pevehouse (2005).

All three types of military interventions show no statistical relationship with democratic transitions. This is in line with previous studies on the topic that have found very little systematic support for external interventions on democratization (De Mesquita and Downs 2006; Downes and Monten 2013; Pickering and Peceny 2006). Finally, we fail to find consistent support for the PTAs, naming and shaming which is largely consistent with existing literature (Gassebner, Lamla, and Vreeland 2013). Variables concerning the international community are found to be less important for understanding state repression than most have suggested when considering direct as well as indirect effects.

3.6.1 Substantive Effects

The impact of the variables identified above for the democratization model are useful to consider but (as above) it is also useful to consider their substantive influence. As found, autocratic governments from the poorest governments have about a 10 percent change of democratizing, however, this drops to a near zero chance for the wealthiest countries. We see similar results for the population measure. Governments from low population governments have about a 22 percent probability of undergoing a democratic transition, but this goes to near zero for the most populous governments. We see that civil war termination has a strong substantive impact on democratization as well. Here, when an autocratic government recently terminated a civil war, the predicted probability increases from about 7 to 24 percent.[56] Governments without a history of regime transitions only have about a 11 percent probability of democratization, but this increases to 60 percent for

[56] We observe a large confidence interval around the predicted probability for civil war termination. This is largely due to the relatively small number of observations that involve both civil war termination and democratization.

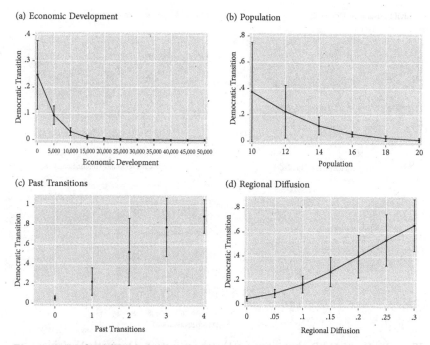

Fig. 3.11 Predicted Probabilities for Democratization, Control Variables

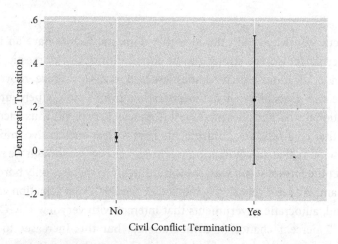

Fig. 3.12 Civil War Termination

governments with a history of transitions. Regional diffusion of democratization is also important, as the predicted probability of a democratic transition increases from about 10 to 40 percent when the number of regional instances of democratization increases!

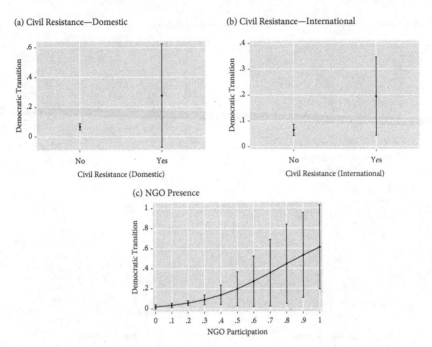

Fig. 3.13 Predicted Probabilities for Democratization, Domestic Variables

Directly consistent with the idea that domestic factors have an impact on governance, we see strong results for the impact of domestic factors on democratization. Purely domestic-based civil resistance movements increase the probability of democratization from 7 to 26 percent while internationally backed ones increase it from 6 to 20 percent. Thus once more, we see that civil resistance movements have a clear substantive impact on the probability that an autocratic government changes, although we need to interpret the former result with some caution given that it is only borderline significant. We see a very strong impact for the INGO participation variable. As found, autocratic governments that interact with very few INGOs have only a 5 percent chance of democratizing, but this increases to about 35 percent for governments with the highest number of INGOs! Again, this indicates that civil society (especially those with strong connections to the international community and other governments) has a substantively meaningful impact on democratic transitions.

Finally, the statistical results suggest that international law is associated with democratic transitions but we see a small substantive impact for this variable. Specifically, governments that have refrained from ratifying the major human rights treaties have a 5 percent probability of democratizing but this increases to 6 percent when a government has a ratified at least one of these treaties.

3.7 What Have We Learned about Spell Onset?

From our investigation into the initiation of LSSR spells from lower levels of government repression as well as from situations where governments have moved from the lowest levels of repression into a slightly higher level before beginning an LSSR, several important insights emerge.

First, it is clear that our theoretical argument has generally received support with domestically oriented variables being statistically as well as substantively more important than internationally oriented ones and political variables like democracy and democratization maintaining the most prominent position within established models.

Second, electoral costs are believed to be the most important. Governments from established electoral democratic systems and newly established ones are less likely to initiate LSSR spells. While the finding concerning levels of democracy is largely consistent with the existing literature on

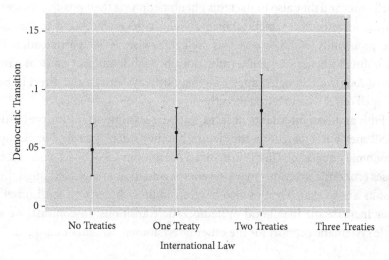

Fig. 3.14 Predicted Probability for Democratization, Human Rights Treaty (International Variable)

state repression/human rights violation, the finding concerning democratic change is a new insight as extant literature largely ignores it. In contrast to the prior literature, we see that judicial democratic institutions are negative in their effects (as expected) but they just miss statistical significance. Nonetheless, these institutions appear to have an indirect impact on termination via its impact on democratization.

Third, the leading independent variables from the variation approach to the study of state repression perform quite well with a few exceptions. Specifically, civil war and population are associated with a higher likelihood of spell onset, while economic development is linked with a smaller probability of it. Youth bulges fail to reach significance in the models, suggesting an important area for future research. This suggests that many of the core findings around which the scholarship on government repression work over the last 50 years extend to a unique reconceptualization of the relevant phenomenon but not all of them.

Fourth, variables that combine domestic-international factors appear to be important for understanding LSSR onset. For example, domestic nonviolent movements that are linked with the larger international community influence this phase of large-scale and violent government behavior although the result is not consistently significant. The empirical findings indicate an important indirect role for global engagement: in particular, internationally backed civil resistance movements are associated with a lower probability of spell onset and they also impact this phenomenon via their positive influence on democratization which (shown above) is generally found to decrease the probability of LSSR onset as well. Likewise, NGO participation has an indirect impact on spell termination through its impact on democratic transitions even though it appears to have little systematic and direct impact on spell onset when viewed directly.

Fifth and last, international factors appear less important for preventing LSSR spell onset than domestic factors, but they still play a role. For example, economic integration (in the form of PTAs) inhibits LSSR onset, and in some cases economic sanctions may prevent the initiation of spells although these results are weaker. Treaties also have an indirect impact on spell onset as they increase the likelihood of democratic transitions. In contrast, we see little systematic support for the other international variables examined.

4

Escalating Spells

4.1 Introduction

Once a government has moved from lower level repressive behavior (PTS 1 and 2) into an LSSR spell, the use of coercion and force is not static. As discussed earlier, spells start when a government receives at least a "3" on the Political Terror Scale but recall that this measure ranges from 1 to 5. Once in a spell, it is possible for repressive behavior to move between 3 and 5—escalating (moving up) or de-escalating (moving down) within this range while the same spell is underway. Acknowledging that individuals and institutions with an interest in reducing state violence might not be able to prevent such activity from beginning in the first place, it would be useful to know how to prevent further escalation.

To explore this topic, we examine a total of 2,539 observations or spell-years and we use the ordered probit estimator to examine escalation. This is done because the dependent variable that ranges from 3 to 5 is ordered in nature (i.e., the categories are arranged in a particular sequence). Following the last chapter, in an effort to assess the substantive impacts of the statistically significant variables, we present the predicated probabilities across all three levels of the PTS (3, 4, and 5).

4.2 Results for Control Variables

In many respects, the findings regarding the influence of standard control variables on spell escalation are comparable to the those obtained from the examination of spell onset. For example, results disclose that when a government is engulfed in ongoing civil war, the predicted probability that it engages in medium levels of repression within a spell (PTS=3) decreases from 64 percent to 28 percent. The predicted probability decreases because governments are more likely to employ higher levels of repression when they are in an ongoing large-scale conflagration. In particular, active civil wars

The Death and Life of State Repression: Understanding Onset, Escalation, Termination, and Recurrence.
Christian Davenport and Benjamin J. Appel, Oxford University Press. © Oxford University Press 2022.
DOI: 10.1093/oso/9780197655375.003.0005

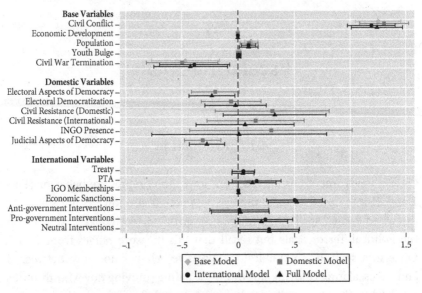

N=2,457. Time and constant variables omitted.
Robust standard errors, clustered on country.

Fig. 4.1 Determinants of Large-Scale, Severe Repression Spell Escalation, 1976–2006

increase the predicted probability that a government employs medium-high levels of repression within a spell (PTS=4) from 23 percent to 42 percent, while it increases the probability that government utilizes the highest forms of repression (PTS=5) by 25 percent, moving it from 4 percent to 29 percent. This suggests (again) that civil war has both a strong statistical and substantive impact on large-scale violent repression by prompting governments to increase the lethality with which they repress.

Related, we find that governments are less likely to escalate repression within a spell following the termination of civil wars. In particular, the cessation of this form of political violence increases the predicted probability that a government uses medium levels of repression by about 7 percent, going from 52 percent to 58 percent. On the other hand, civil war termination decreases the predicted probability of the two highest forms of repression; i.e., medium-high repression drops from 29 percent to 23 percent, while the highest level of repression likewise declines from about 13 percent to 8 percent. With less of an obvious reason for ramping up repressive behavior (i.e., behavioral challenges), nation–states are less likely to see more violence.

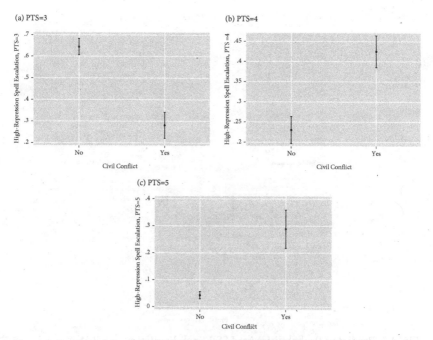

Fig. 4.2 Predicted Probabilities for LSSR Spell Escalation, Civil War

In line with our expectations and those of the literature, the population variable is statistically significant. At medium-levels of repressive behavior (level 3), the predicted probability decreases from about 60 percent to 49 percent as population increases from low to high levels. The probability that a government with a relatively small population escalates to the medium-high levels of repressive behavior (PTS=4) is 20 percent but this increases to 33 percent for the most populous governments. Likewise, the predicted probability of escalating repression within a spell increases from 6 to 18 percent at the highest levels of repression (PTS=5) as population likewise increases. This suggests (once more) that population and the difficulties of controlling large numbers of people are generally associated with higher levels of repressive behavior/human rights violation.

Regarding other contextual factors, we see little support for youth bulges and economic development. Once an LSSR is underway, the demographic balance within the relevant population and the economic resources available to political authorities appear to be irrelevant. Again, this is a significant difference from variation research which has consistently found these factors to be important.

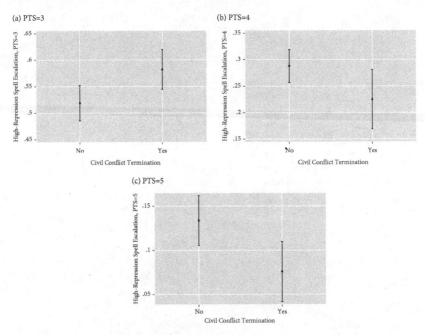

Fig. 4.3 Predicted Probabilities for LSSR Spell Escalation, Civil War Termination

4.3 Results for Domestic Variables

Investigating the influence of domestic factors, we see the relevant measures produce some interesting results. For example, it is found that the level of democracy is negative and statistically significant, suggesting that governments of this type are less inclined to escalate repression once an LSSR is underway—compared to nondemocratic governments. Regarding the substantive impact, democracy increases the predicted probability that a regime engages in medium-repression from about 51 percent to 56 percent. Democratic government decreases the likelihood of medium-high repression, moving the predicted probability from 30 percent to 26 percent, while it decreases the likelihood of government engages in the highest levels of repression from about 14 to 10 percent. Taken together, the findings indicate that, in addition to preventing LSSRs from starting, democracy reduces the likelihood that government will escalate repression to the highest levels—even in the context of LSSR spells. Such a finding further attests to the ability of electoral institutions to constrain repressive governments! This said, the effects are not as large as we expected and thus

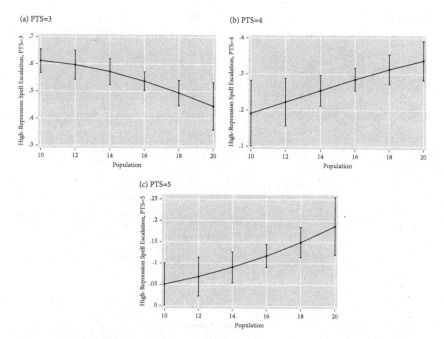

Fig. 4.4 Predicted Probabilities for LSSR Spell Escalation, Population

it is revealed that the domestic democratic peace is a partial solution to the problem of escalation but not a perfect one.

In line with expectations, consistent results are found for the other domestic-oriented variables. Further speaking to the importance of the domestic democratic peace proposition, judicial aspects of democracy are found to be negative and statistically significant in their impact, indicating that independent judiciaries can constrain governments from further ramping up repressive behavior after spells have already been initiated. In the presence of independent judiciaries, the predicted probability of medium-repression (PTS=3) increases from 50 percent to 56 percent. Contrasting this, independent judiciaries decrease the predicted probability for medium-high repression from 31 to 26 percent. Finally, in the absence of an effective and independent judiciary, the predicated probability that repressive behavior escalates to the highest levels (of PTS=5) is 15 percent but this drops to 9 percent when the government has a strong judiciary.

Related, we see that electoral democratization is negative in its impact on escalation but that it fails to reach standard levels of significance. This suggests that democratic transitions involving electoral dimensions have a

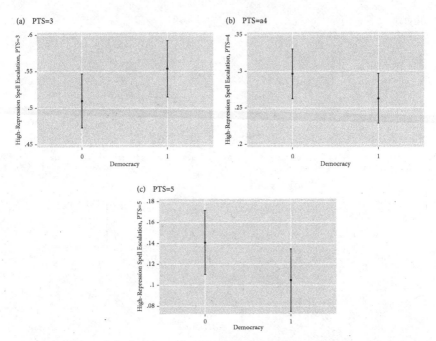

Fig. 4.5 Predicted Probabilities for LSSR Spell Escalation, Democracy

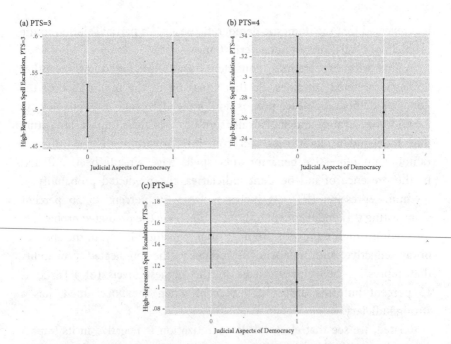

Fig. 4.6 Predicted Probabilities for LSSR Spell Escalation, Judicial Aspects of Democracy

pacifying impact on LSSR because it helps to prevent its occurrence in the first place but it cannot stop authorities from escalating related coercion and force once a spell has been initiated!

Finally, we see little (direct) influence regarding domestic groups in LSSR spells. The civil resistance measure that involves external support and the NGO variable both fail to reach standard levels of significance which is largely consistent with the primary set of findings.

4.4 Results for International Variables

Examining policies/variables that are more international in nature, the models produce some important results. For example, we observe little systematic support for the impact of the international "carrot" measures on the escalation of repression within a spell. As found, signing/ratifying treaties, PTAs, and IGO membership all fail to reach standard levels of statistical significance. Once large-scale, severe repression is underway, there is very little that can be done by the international community (in terms of their standard repertoire) to induce political authorities away from engaging in worse human rights abuses!

At the same time, we also see that many "stick" variables are associated with the escalation of repressive behavior during spells. We believe this is because the phenomena of interest represent a threat to political authorities who are already feeling vulnerable—this reveals the dynamics of building momentum within the spell discussed in the theory section. For example, economic sanctions, pro-government interventions, and neutral interventions are all positive and statistically significant in their impact on escalation, although pro-government interventions are only borderline significant. In contrast, the anti-government intervention variable is positive but fails to reach standard levels of significance. With regard to substantive impact, economic sanctions decrease the predicted probability of medium repression from 54 percent to 42 percent. In the absence of sanctions, the predicted probability for medium-high repression is 28 percent but this increases to 35 percent once sanctions are enacted. Economic sanctions increase the predicted probability of the worst form of repression by about 10 percentage points, increasing the probability from 11 to 21 percent in the context of a spell. Similarly, neutral interventions decrease the predicted probability of medium repression from 53 percent to 47 percent when a spell is underway.

Interventions of this type increase the two highest levels of repression from 28 to 32 percent and 12 to 17 percent, respectively.

4.5 What Have We Learned?

From our investigation into the escalation of an LSSR, we are once more provided with numerous insights into government repression.

First, results disclose that there are numerous factors associated with the escalation of ongoing large-scale, severe repression which are directly in line with our juggernaut theory.

Second, electoral and judicial aspects of democracy are associated with a lower probability that governments escalate repression within already initiated LSSRs. However, and in contrast to the results from the onset model, results disclose that democratization does not hinder escalation.

Third, civil war termination provides another way to diminish the probability of escalating LSSRs. As found, when this form of conflagration is ended, the likelihood of political authorities increasing the scale and scope

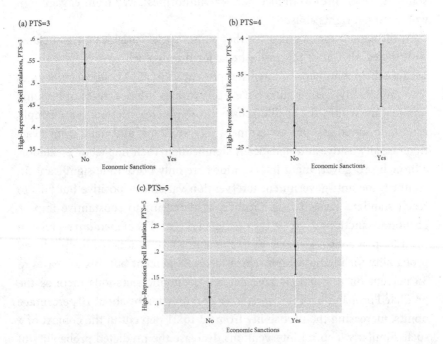

Fig. 4.7 Predicted Probabilities for LSSR Spell Escalation, Economic Sanctions

of repressive behavior is diminished. The results indicate that policymakers, activists, and advocates could focus on ending civil wars if they want to help decrease the chances that large-scale, violent repression is increased further. To be clear, this does not mean that repressive spells end, which will be discussed below. Rather, it means that repressive behavior within a spell is not increased in severity and scope.

Fourth, we find that international variables have little impact on spell escalation, and in some cases they appear to make things worse. In particular, pro-government as well as neutral military interventions and economic sanctions lead to the escalation of repression when LSSRs are underway. This indicates that typically these go-to foreign policy tools are actually counter-productive in bringing about frequently desired outcome concerning non-escalation, at least in the context of ongoing LSSRs. These results are especially important to take note of because they suggest that international sticks have a counter-productive impact on the severity/scope of repression even in LSSR spells. In contrast to their objective to help reduce state repressive behavior, these foreign policy tools consistently

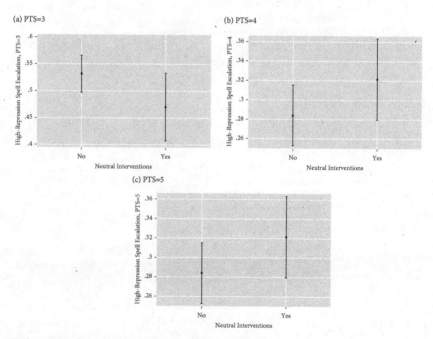

Fig. 4.8 Predicted Probabilities for LSSR Spell Escalation, Neutral Interventions

worsen the human rights practices of repressive governments! This is an especially useful finding because political advocates and academics often call for such responses in the midst of state violence.

Fifth and lastly, we observe that ongoing civil war, population, and youth bulges are all still associated with an increased probability that LSSRs will escalate after they have been initiated. As such, the standard factors highlighted by the repression literature are still related and in the expected ways.

5

Ending Spells

5.1 Introduction

Having now discussed the onset of LSSRs, the onset of an LSSR given a prior low-level escalation in repressive behavior before onset as well as escalation within an LSSR once it is underway, in this chapter we move to address the question that motivated us to write the book that you are currently reading: what stops large-scale government repressive behavior that is ongoing?

As you may recall, our theoretical argument suggested that once up and running, LSSRs would be hard to stop through the imposition of costs—that is unless the costs were significant enough to disturb the repressive process. Such an orientation significantly reduces the number of factors we thought would be relevant and, indeed, such an orientation suggests that only a few would be likely to wield impactful costs—i.e., political democracy and democratization. With this in mind, we move to our empirical investigation.

Earlier, we identified that the threshold used to determine the onset of a spell is a PTS score of "3" or more where repression becomes violent, institutionalized, and carried out systematically across large parts of a population. This status is maintained until the PTS drops below "3" for at least two consecutive years. With this conceptualization, the data contains a total of 145 terminations (across 150 countries for the period between 1976 and 2006) out of 244 total spells.

Consistent with the onset analysis, we estimate four models to assess our theoretical framework:[57] first, a baseline model is estimated that only includes the standard control variables from the literature. We then estimate a model for domestic variables, domestic-international hybrids plus controls variables and then a model for the international variables

---

[57] In order to test our theoretical argument, we employ a discrete time duration model with logistic regression and a counter of time. We also use robust standard errors to deal with serial correlation, clustered on the spell.

The Death and Life of State Repression: Understanding Onset, Escalation, Termination, and Recurrence.
Christian Davenport and Benjamin J. Appel, Oxford University Press. © Oxford University Press 2022.
DOI: 10.1093/oso/9780197655375.003.0006

domestic-international hybrids plus the controls. Finally, the full model is presented that includes the control variables, and domestic variables, international variables as well as domestic-international hybrids.

5.2 Results for Control Variables

From our analysis, we find that the control variables are largely consistent with prior research (based on the variation approach) as well as the three previous investigations estimated in earlier chapters.

Consistent with expectations, ongoing civil war is positive and significant in its impact on LSSR termination indicating that as long as these forms of political violence are underway LSSRs are less likely to end. Substantively, civil war decreases the probability that a spell terminates from 7 to about 2 percent. In contrast, civil war termination has a strong and positive impact on spell termination. In particular, the probability that a government ends an LSSR is about 10 percentage points higher (5 to 15 percent) when a civil war ended. Put differently, civil war termination increases the probability of

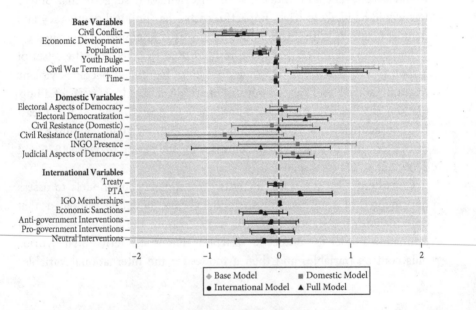

N=2,282. Time and constant variables omitted.
Robust standard errors, clustered on country.

Fig. 5.1 Determinants of LSSR Spell Termination, 1976–2006

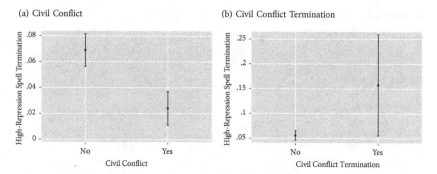

Fig. 5.2 Predicted Probabilities for LSSR Spell Termination, Control Variables

spell termination by about 200 percent! Clearly this variable is important but what is also worthy of note is that it does not completely account for the end of a repressive spell. Other factors are relevant.

Consistent with prior research, more populous countries are associated with longer spells. The predicted probability that a government ends an LSSR decreases from about 20 percent in low-population countries to 2 percent in high-population ones. In contrast to the onset model, here the youth bulge measure is negative and statistically significant. This indicates that despite their irrelevance for LSSR onset and escalation, large youth bulges decrease the likelihood that governments terminate spells that are already underway. Substantively, when the youth bulge is small, the predicted probability that a government terminates an LSSR is about 15 percent but this decreases to 3 percent for very large cohorts. This demonstrates that population-based pressures do indeed have a impact on repressive behavior but only for specific phases of the repressive life cycle—a finding that was not previously possible to detect because of the aggregation across distinct phases.

Finally, we observe that the linear counter of time has a negative and statistically significant impact on spell termination. Such a finding suggests that longer spells are less likely to end compared to shorter ones. Directly supporting our primary theoretical insight about stickiness and momentum, this indicates that spells do indeed become increasingly harder to end as they persist. Supportive finding aside, the influence is admittedly lower than anticipated. Regarding the substantive impact, the predicted probability that a spell terminates after one year is about 9 percent, but this decreases to about 6 percent after 5 years, 3 percent after 10 years, and 1 percent after

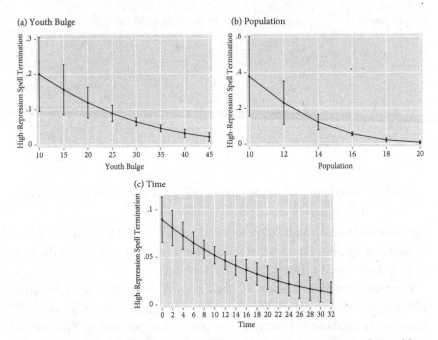

Fig. 5.3 Predicted Probabilities for LSSR Spell Termination, Control Variables

30 years. While momentum and stickiness pay a role, therefore, it is not an all-powerful deterrent and assured pathway to peace.

5.3 Results for Domestic Variables

We next turn to a discussion of the domestic variables which produce some important as well as surprising results. First, the judicial aspects of democracy are positive and statistically significant in both models, although it is only weakly significant in the domestic-politics model. From our analyses, strong rule of law governments are likely to have shorter spells, which is largely consistent with existing variation research as it highlights the pacifying influence of democratic political systems. Substantively, the probability that a government terminates an LSSR is only about 4 percent when it lacks strong judicial constraints, but this increases to about 7 percent in the presence of an independent judiciary.

Electoral aspects of democratization consistently influence LSSR spell termination as they are positive and statistically significant in both models.

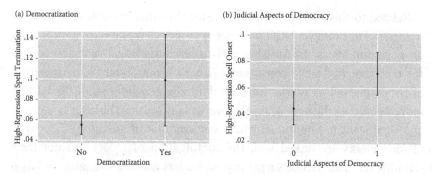

Fig. 5.4 Predicted Probabilities for LSSR Spell Termination, Domestic Variables

Here, autocratic governments have about a 5 percent chance of terminating an LSSR spell, but this increases to about 10 percent following a democratic transition. Newly democratic governments therefore are about 100 percent more likely to end a spell compared to the previous autocratic regime. This finding is in line with our theoretical argument that it takes a fundamental shift to the political apparatus to stop governments from continuing to violently violate human rights on a large scale. Democratization appears to satisfy this important condition by changing who is in charge of the government, establishing electoral accountability as well as facilitating mass participation in the political process. The substantive power of this influence is perhaps less than many (including us) would like but the impact is nevertheless worthy of attention.

In contrast to the impact of democratization, the level of electoral democracy is positive in its effect on spell termination (as expected) but it fails to reach standard levels of significance (which given the prominence of this variable in the literature we did not anticipate). While this is inconsistent with much of the research on repression/human rights violation, it makes sense in the context of the current study because we maintain that it takes a major disturbance to terminate government use of LSSR and a pre-existing democratic political system (even in the minimal sense) does not represent a disruption but rather a stable pattern of government. There is also likely a selection effect in that (as we identified earlier) strong democracies are less likely to find themselves in LSSR spells in the first place. As a result, democracies that do engage in LSSR consist of a sub-sample of all democratic governments.

Related to this, we see little support for the other variables classified as domestic. For example, NGO presence appears to have no systematic impact on governments as the variable fails to reach statistical significance. We see that civil resistance consistently fails to bring about the termination of LSSR spells. This is true for both domestic and internationally backed movements (i.e., the hybrid). In fact, we actually see that the latter is negative and significant in one model which suggests that (if anything) these type of movements are linked with the continuation of LSSRs and not their termination. This is not surprising, as leaders already engaging in large-scale, severe repression likely view civil resistance movements as a threat and thus are inclined to continue or perhaps even ramp up their repressive activities. This is significantly at odds with some research however which suggests that these movements are important for bringing about diverse socio-political outcomes that are generally considered desirable—such as ending state repression (Stephan and Chenoweth 2008; Chenoweth, Stephan, and Stephan 2011). We discuss this further below.

5.4 Results for International Variables

Further supporting our theoretical argument, we see very little support for the internationally oriented variables and relevant hybrids typically highlighted in the literature. For example, Preferential Trade Agreements (while positive) fail to reach standard levels of significance. Likewise, the ratification of human rights treaty fails to come close to significance. Once more, all three military intervention variables fail to achieve statistical significance, which indicates the ineffectiveness of military interventions at the times they are frequently believed to be needed most. Finally, economic sanctions produce inconsistent results across the models estimated.

This said, not all internationally oriented variables are unimportant. In contrast to the results identified above from other phases of the repressive life cycle, we do see some support for the IGO membership variable. This is positive and statistically significant, suggesting that repressive governments are more inclined to terminate their large-scale and violent behavior when they are diplomatically integrated into the international community-making them more susceptible to certain types of pressure (i.e., costs). Substantively, the probability that a repressive regime with a low number of IGO member-ships terminates its behavior is about 3 percent but this increases to about

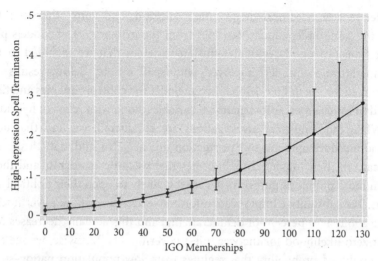

Fig. 5.5 Predicted Probabilities for LSSR Spell Termination, International Variables

11 percent for governments that have a high number of IGO memberships. The idea here is that political authorities are unlikely to engage in repression when they are subject to the scrutiny and normative expectations of their peers. This is especially interesting because the IGO variable was not shown to effect onset or escalation. While this result is at odds with some research, other scholars find some support for the role of IGOs (Greenhill 2010). Our finding suggests that both were right—IGOs are just relevant for particular phases of the larger repressive life cycle like youth bulges![58]

5.5 The Determinants of Electoral Democratization

In line with our other analyses above as well as our desire to assist those interested with ending state repressive spells, we continue to recognize the substantive importance of electoral democratization to LSSRs and offer an investigation of what influences shifts in democracy where LSSRs are already underway. Commensurate with our earlier analyses, we estimate our model on a sample of nondemocratic governments. We create a new response variable that equals "1" if the government recently

[58] It is important to note that the IGO membership measure fails to reach significance in the fixed effects model reported in the appendix.

underwent an electoral democratic transition, and zero otherwise. We use the same independent variables from the primary set of models plus past transitions and regional diffusion variables that we included in the democratization model employed with spell onsets. Below, results are presented for the full model that first includes the control variables and then the domestic as well as international variables along with relevant hybrids.

When our empirical investigations are conducted, we find that both economic development and population are negative and statistically significant in their impact. This indicates that wealthier autocrats and those from more populous governments are less likely to open their political systems. The substantive impacts are informative. Relatively poor governments have about a 10 percent of democratizing, and this actually decreases to a near zero likelihood for the wealthiest governments. Likewise, we see that the predicted probability that regimes from low-population nation-states democratize is about 20 percent and this decreases to about 4 percent for highly populous nation-states.

In contrast to earlier findings, we observe that civil war is linked with a greater likelihood of democratization but it is only borderline

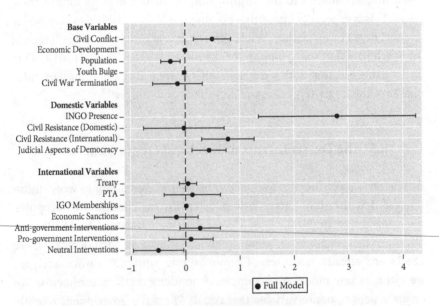

N=1,782. Time and constant variables omitted.
Robust standard errors, clustered on country.

Fig. 5.6 Determinants of Democratization in LSSR Spells, 1976–2006

statistically significant. Ongoing civil conflicts increase the probability of democratic transitions from about 8 to 11 percent. While potentially surprising, it is important to recall that these conflicts are taking place in the context of authoritarianism and thus it is possible that governments experience a regime-change during civil wars which might ultimately lead to democratization. These outcomes are often the objective of such conflicts. We discuss this further in the next chapter.

The last contextual variables that are statistically significant include prior experience with democratization as well as regional diffusion. As found, governments without a history of democratization have about a 6 percent probability of democratizing, but this increases to about 65 percent for governments with a history of them! Likewise, higher levels of regional diffusion of democratic transitions increase the predicted probability of democratization in the government from about 5 to 65 percent. This significant finding reveals the importance of democratization as an institution of peace-making with regionally transformative events. It literally seems to take a global village to facilitate change.

Considering domestic and domestic-international hybrid variables, again the domestic variables produce a strong set of results. For example, we see that judicial aspects of democracy serve as an important foundation upon which electoral democracy can rise. When the government lacks an independent judiciary, its probability of democratizing is about 6 percent but this increases to 13 percent when there are strong judicial checks. Governments with civil society movements that are connected to the larger international community (a domestic-international hybrid) tend to be more likely to democratize as well. Such a consideration increases the predicted probability of a democratic transition from 3 to 38 percent, which is quite powerful relative to other influences.

Similarly, international-backed civil resistance movements (another domestic-international hybrid) are associated with a greater likelihood of democratic transition. The probability that a repressive, autocrat democratizes is about 8 percent in the absence of an internationally supported civil resistance movement, but this increases to about 18 percent in the presence of one. This indicates that substantive importance for these types of movements is actually quite meaningful as they increase the probability of a democratic transition by over 200 percent! Interestingly and directly moving against this finding, however, results disclose the civil resistance movements which are not backed by international actors have no impact at all.

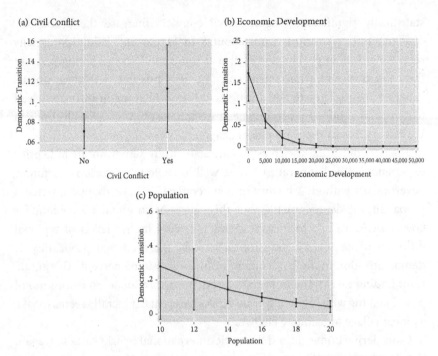

Fig. 5.7 Predicted Probabilities for Democratization in LSSR Spells, Control Variables

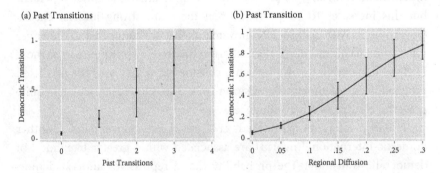

Fig. 5.8 Predicted Probabilities for Democratization in LSSR Spells, Control Variables

Consistent with earlier findings, international variables show little systematic impact on democratization. For example, treaties, PTAs, IGO membership, and economic sanctions all fail to reach standard levels of significance. Related to this, we see little support for the military intervention variables.

This is in line with previous studies on the topic that find little support for the impact of external interventions on democratization (De Mesquita and Downs 2006; Downes and Monten 2013; Pickering and Peceny 2006).

5.6 What Have We Learned?

From our investigation into the factors that stop an ongoing large-scale, violent spell, we have advanced existing knowledge in numerous ways.

First, summarily considering all variables together, we see there are few factors that are consistently associated with stopping LSSRs. Within baseline models, civil war termination and democratic institutions appear to be the best ways to end these events. While the civil war termination finding provides support to arguments based on the law of coercive threats and offers an alternative pathway to exiting LSSRs, the political democratization finding lends strong support for our juggernaut theoretical argument. Interestingly, the level of democracy is associated with a lower probability that

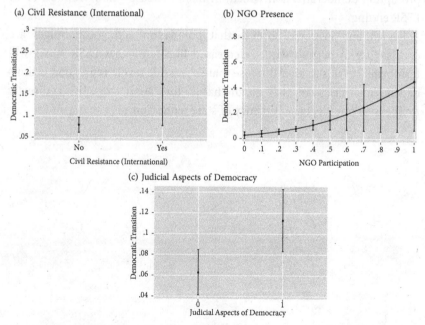

Fig. 5.9 Predicted Probabilities for Democratization in LSSR Spells, Domestic Variables

governments escalate LSSR, although it does not appear to be linked with its termination.

Second, while not having a direct impact on repressive behavior, domestic movements backed by international actors can assist with ending LSSR by increasing the likelihood that repressive governments democratize. This adds nuance to our theoretical argument by adding an indirect path to pacification.

Third, from our empirical investigations, international variables have little direct impact on spell termination, and they, in some cases, appear to exacerbate repressive behavior. In particular, international "sticks" such as military interventions and economic sanctions prolong spells. This indicates that in the context of LSSR these foreign policy tools are counter-productive! IGO membership does appear to be associated with termination, suggesting an important avenue for later research to assess the robustness of this finding and to better identify the precise causal mechanisms driving the relationship. Finally, there appears to be an indirect role for the international community to play on spell termination through civil resistance movements. For example, those that receive external support tend to have a higher likelihood of prompting democratization which, in turn, increases the likelihood of an LSSR ending.

Fourth and last, we observe that population and youth bulges are consistently associated with a decreased likelihood that LSSR spells will terminate. Results further disclose that large-scale severe repression is time-dependent—the longer they go, the harder they are to stop. This is directly in line with our juggernaut theory of state repression.

6

Recurring Spells

6.1 Introduction

In this chapter, we end our statistical investigation of repressive spells by considering those circumstances when a country that previously had an LSSR has another one (i.e., those that recur). Scholars working in related literatures such as civil war, find that these types of political conflagrations recur about 50 percent of the time (Loyle and Appel 2017; David Mason et al. 2011). Because of this realization, understanding the factors associated with preventing their recurrence has become an important avenue of research and public policy. The same logic applies to our interest in repression spells. Differing from other forms, we find that LSSR spells recur about 40 percent of the time, suggesting that this is indeed an important phenomenon to understand but not as bad as some other forms of large-scale political violence. Along with investigations of LSSR onset, escalation, and termination, however, this topic has not previously been examined. We (again) offer the first exploration of the subject below.

To address this line of inquiry, we restrict our analysis to governments that previously experienced an LSSR. Within this sample of governments, spells recur 101 times from 1976 to 2006 across 1,015 observations. In line with earlier analyses, we estimate four models: (1) a baseline model, (2) a domestic model, (3) an international model, and (4) a full model. The final response variable (recurrence) in this analysis equals 1 when an LSSR spell recurs, and zero otherwise.

Recall that our theoretical discussion leads us to anticipate that recurrence will potentially reveal a unique set of determinants compared to the other stages of LSSR. This was expected because prior LSSRs take a toll on all parties involved and the degree to which the repressive cohort has been disturbed directly influences what subsequently transpires.

The Death and Life of State Repression: Understanding Onset, Escalation, Termination, and Recurrence.
Christian Davenport and Benjamin J. Appel, Oxford University Press. © Oxford University Press 2022.
DOI: 10.1093/oso/9780197655375.003.0007

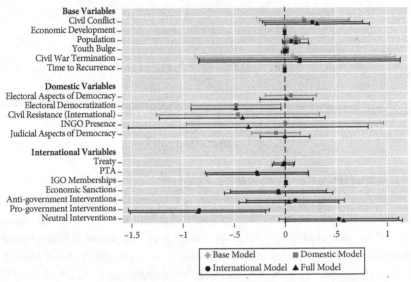

N=834. Time and constant variables omitted.
Robust standard errors, clustered on country.

Fig. 6.1 Determinants of LSSR Spell Recurrence, 1976–2006

6.2 Results for Control Variables

Different from the other analyses provided within earlier chapters, we see mixed results for the leading control variables in the literature when recurrence is considered. For example, reflecting the idea of war-weariness, we observe that ongoing civil war is positive in that it tends to increase the likelihood that LSSRs recur but it fails to reach standard levels of significance. Large-scale behavioral challenges therefore do not generally lead political authorities to engage in LSSR after they have already done so! On the other hand, economic development is negative and statistically significant. The probability that a poor government initiates another LSSR spell is about 10 percent but this drops to about zero percent for wealthier governments. Consistent with the results from the onset model, this indicates that governments are less inclined to employ LSSR when their economies are strong and options for state-sponsored socio-political control exist.

Supportive of the larger literature on government repression, we (again) see that governments ruling over more populous countries are more likely to return to LSSR spells although this result is borderline significant. The threats presented by these socio-political problems lead authorities to engage

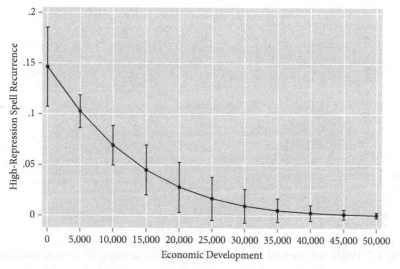

Fig. 6.2 Predicted Probabilities for LSSR Spell Recurrence, Control Variables

in repressive action against large parts of the relevant population. Similar to earlier analyses, results disclose that both youth bulges and civil war termination are in the expected direction but fail to reach statistical significance. Finally, we see that the linear counter of time is positive but it fails to reach standard levels of significance.

6.3 Results for Domestic Variables

In Figure 6.1, we report the results for the domestic-based variables along with relevant domestic-international hybrids. From this investigation, we observe that electoral democracy fails to reach standard levels of significance. This is somewhat surprising to us. Given our theoretical argument concerning repressive cohorts and momentum, there is little reason to expect that electoral democratic processes constrain democratic governments from employing LSSR when they previously failed to do so. Interestingly, we see a similar result for the judicial aspect of political democracy. Within our analysis, this variable is negative but it fails to reach standard levels of statistical significance. Given the power inherent within distinct aspects of democracy, if elections did not wield an influence it makes sense that the judiciary would not prevent democratic governments from engaging in LSSR when it failed to stop them earlier. Taken together, this suggests that repressive democratic

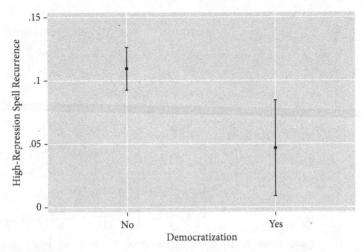

Fig. 6.3 Predicted Probabilities for LSSR Spell Recurrence, Domestic Variables

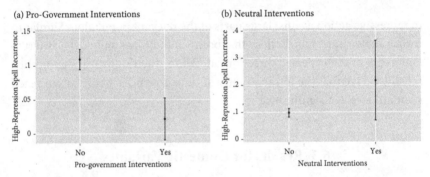

Fig. 6.4 Predicted Probabilities for LSSR Recurrence, International Variables

governments represent a distinct type of democracy that is unconstrained by the usual pacifying mechanisms traditionally highlighted. Indeed, in line with our theoretical argument, it suggests that once a government has explained/justified repression to itself, it would unlikely be pressured to change that position. This represents an incredibly important exception to the domestic democratic peace and, in line with the use of repression during the post-911 era as well as the recent Trump administration, it is clear that this topic of recurring democratic repression is worthy of additional consideration in the future.

In contrast to the results just discussed, we again see that political democratization is negative and statistically significant in its impact. This suggests that recently democratized governments are less likely to renew spells of LSSR against those within their territorial jurisdiction. Once again, as the probability that a repressive autocratic regime initiates another LSSR spell after having had one already is about 11 percent, this decreases to 4 percent when the government recently democratized. This result provides additional support for our juggernaut theoretical argument that it takes a major shift within the government to prevent political authorities from again using large-scale repression.

Differing from earlier chapters, we see little direct support for the domestic mobilization variables, as even those that are backed by international actors are negative but fail to reach standard levels of significance. Recurrent LSSRs appear to represent a very different situation from the other phases of the repressive life cycle discussed above.

6.4 Results for International Variables

In line with our theory and most of the analyses observed earlier, we again found weak support for the role played by international variables in the study of recurrence. For example, both PTAs and economic sanctions are not significant in the model, suggesting that international economic factors have little systematic impact on whether governments renew LSSRs. Results disclose that human rights treaties and IGO membership have no impact on recurrence. This suggests that international law and politics are unimportant as well.

Again, not all international variables are deemed irrelevant. Interestingly, we see that the pro-government interventions variable is negative and significant. A repressive regime without a pro-government military intervention has about a 10 percent chance of starting an LSSR spell, but this drops to about 2 percent chance when there has been a pro-government intervention. This suggests that governments that experience these types of interventions are less likely to resume LSSRs. One could explain the finding by working the increased capabilities that these types of interventions bring to the relevant government and that this might reduce the perception of threat as well as the perceived necessity for repressive behavior. Such a topic could benefit from additional consideration in the future.

In contrast to this result, we see no systematic support for anti-government interventions on recurrence but we observe that neutral interventions are linked with a higher probability of spell recurrence as they increase the predicted probability of this taking place from about 10 to 20 percent. Contrasting prior research, therefore, we observe that interventions which are affiliated with no side in particular have a counter-productive impact on LSSR spells occurring after one has already happened!

6.5 The Determinants of Electoral Democratization

Faced with another statistically as well as substantively important impact of democratization, we once again explore what influences this shift in government. In Figure 6.1, we present the results for the democratization model based on the recurrence sample. Overall, the model produces findings that are largely consistent with earlier analyses.

For example, controls look relatively similar to what was identified in the chapters examined previously. We see that ongoing civil war is associated with a greater probability of electoral democratization, suggesting that governments experience liberalizing political changes during ongoing conflict. The predicted probability for democratization increases from 12 percent to 28 percent when a government is involved in an active civil war. In contrast, we see that economic development is linked with a decreased likelihood of democratization. As the economic system develops from low to high, the predicted probability for democratization decreases from about 12 percent to basically zero. Interestingly, youth bulges, population, and civil war termination again reveal no systematic relationship with political democratization.

Along with existing literature, we see that both past transitions and regional diffusion are statistically significant and in the expected direction. Regarding the former, transitions in the past have a large substantive impact on subsequent electoral democratization, moving from about 18 percent for those without a history of them to about 50 percent to those with a history of transitions. Regarding the latter, high numbers of democratic transitions in the region increase the probability of democratic transitions from about 17 percent to 47 percent compared to regions that lack such transitions. Context thus matters a great deal.

Also significant, we see that when the government has previously experienced large-scale, violent repression, internationally backed domestic movements are associated with a higher probability of democratization.

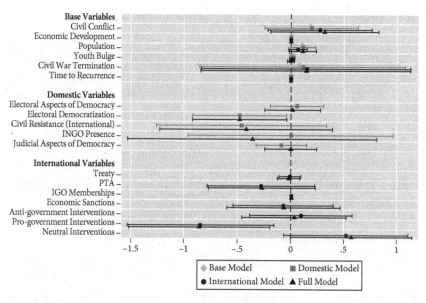

Fig. 6.5 Determinants of Electoral Democratization Following LSSR Spells, 1976–2006

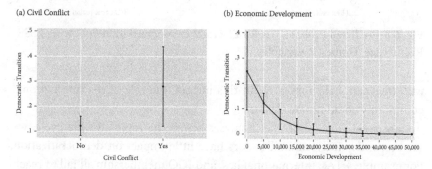

Fig. 6.6 Predicted Probabilities for Electoral Democratization Following LSSR Spell Recurrence, Control Variables

Specifically, governments that are targeted by civil resistance movements with third-party support are more likely to democratize, while they are more inclined to do so when INGO involvement is higher. Substantively, when there is no internationally backed civil resistance movement, the probability that a repressive autocrat democratizes is about 12 percent but this jumps to 24 percent when there is such a civil resistance movement association

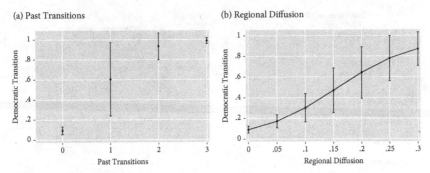

Fig. 6.7 Predicted Probabilities for Electoral Democratization Following LSSR Spell Recurrence, Control Variables

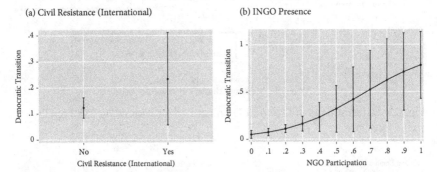

Fig. 6.8 Predicted Probabilities for Electoral Democratization Following LSSR Recurrence, Domestic Variables

with international support. With this impact, the role of the international community could not be clearer.

Consistent with our earlier analyses across the repressive life cycle, we see that many international factors have little impact on democratization. For example, PTAs, international law, and IGO membership all fail to reach statistical significance. Economic sanctions are linked to a lower probability of democratic transitions, decreasing the predicted probability of democratization from about 13 percent to almost zero. This suggests that they have a strong negative impact on the prospects for electoral democratization.

Once again, we see mixed support for the military intervention variables. On the one hand, anti-government interventions and neutral interventions are not significant. On the other hand, pro-government interventions are negative, indicating that they are associated with a lower probability of democratization. Substantively, the predicated probability declines about

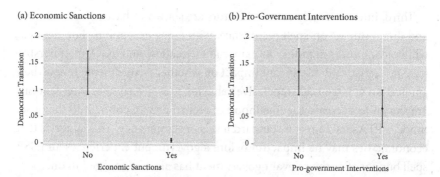

Fig. 6.9 Predicted Probabilities for Electoral Democratization Following LSSR Spell Recurrence, International Variables

6 percent, going from 13 percent to 7 percent in the presence of a pro-government intervention.

6.6 What Have We Learned?

Considering situations where a spell of LSSR has already taken place, we explore what influences the subsequent initiation of another LSSR. When doing this we see that while certain results are shared in common with the other phases of the repressive life cycle, the findings regarding recurrence are somewhat distinct. This is not entirely surprising given that this phenomenon represents a subsample of LSSR onset cases but it is quite informative about what has an impact and when.

First, there are some clear determinants that are consistent with our theoretical argument as well as earlier analyses. For example, results disclose that political democratization decreases the likelihood of spell recurrence. Interestingly, there is no relationship between democracy and the resumption of an LSSR. Finally, civil resistance movements and NGO participation have an indirect impact on recurrence via their impact on democratization but this is conditional on international support.

Second, we see that economic development and population behave as expected—respectively increasing and deceasing the likelihood of recurrence, but youth bulges (again) appear to have no systematic impact on the recurrence of a LSSR. In contrast to our expectations, however, the civil war variable fails to reach standard levels of significance, although it is positive in its effect (as expected).

Third, internationally oriented factors are shown to have little systematic and direct impact on spell recurrence, with a few exceptions. For example, while economic sanctions, human rights treaties, and IGO membership have no statistically significant impact on whether governments renew their application of large-scale repressive behavior, pro-government interventions are shown to decrease the likelihood of recurrence. In contrast to the onset models, PTAs fail to reach standard levels of significance. This suggests that economic ties may be impactful before a government experiences an LSSR spell but not after the relevant government has already engaged in one.

7

Cases

7.1 Introduction

Within the analyses above, we generally found support for our juggernaut theoretical argument across phases of the repressive life cycle—i.e., reducing the likelihood of starting a large-scale repressive spell, escalating one, continuing the spell, as well as preventing a recurrence in a country where one had already occurred. While the importance of different variables appears to vary a little across phases, three appear to be consistently important: electoral democratization, civil resistance, and civil war.

In our statistical investigation, we acknowledge that we did not pay attention to the temporal sequence involved when the three variables took place. Exactly when someone did something to someone else was not as rigorously explored for alternative pathways. In part, this limitation was a function of the type of examinations we estimated which were probabilistic in nature. It is informative, however, to consider the different ways that the three variables of interest occurred sequentially. For example, highlighting our focus on stopping ongoing spells, our theoretical argument as well as most of our empirical results suggest a very specific four-step process exists where 1) a repressive spell is initiated, 2) civil resistance takes place, 3) democratization occurs and 4) the repressive spell ends. Looking at the database and history of the cases involved, it is clear that there are numerous examples of this sequence. This said, our data and history reveal that these are not the only ways that spells can end. For example, it is possible that civil resistance and civil war precede democratization which, in turn, leads to spell termination. Given the nature of the lags we explore, it is also possible that democratization occurs before civil resistance and/or civil war, which in turn precedes spell termination.

Within this chapter, we discuss these diverse situations, highlighting cases drawn from the relevant time period. It should be clear though that we do not engage in this exercise in an effort to challenge or undermine our statistical analysis. Rather, this is done in order to explore the potential complexities

The Death and Life of State Repression: Understanding Onset, Escalation, Termination, and Recurrence.
Christian Davenport and Benjamin J. Appel, Oxford University Press. © Oxford University Press 2022.
DOI: 10.1093/oso/9780197655375.003.0008

that exist within the derived empirical findings—gauging the validity of our effort and guiding future research into the relevant topic.

7.2 Spell Sequence I: Start Spell, Civil Resistance, Democracy, End Spell

As theorized, some of our cases involved an LSSR spell being met with civil resistance and subsequently democratization before the spell was brought to an end. We discuss four below.

7.2.1 Chile, 1976–93

In our data, Chile's repressive spell begins in 1976, but this is largely an artifact of the data. Most likely, repression reached the level of a spell after Socialist President Salvador Allende was overthrown by the military and a junta established a dictatorship in 1973. Although General Augusto Pinochet of the army was perhaps the leading figure in the emerging cohort around the new repressive policy, there were other members: e.g., diverse members of the Navy (who started the idea of the coup), the army, air and police forces, conservative political organizations, the United States government, as well as multinational corporations. This cohort came into being as a critique to economic and political instabilities that began to emerge under Allende. The economic issues involved rising prices, food shortages, calls for higher wages, and general problems with Socialist economic policies from those who were interested in capitalistic development. The political issues concerned numerous strikes from workers, protests from women, and a failed coup from part of the military under Colonel Roberto Souper.

During the years which followed the successful coup, Pinochet consolidated his command and the Chilean government curbed dissent with unprecedented repressive measures targeting leftists and supporters of these ideologies. Politically motivated disappearances in large number began almost from the beginning of the spell as well as arbitrary detention and torture—complete with psychological duress, electric shock and interrogations, and beatings. Describing this period, General Joaquin Lagos Osorio stated that prisoners' bodies were often not returned to their families. He noted the vulgarity of the executions committed, identifying that the security forces were intent on inflicting the maximum amount of pain on societal actors and the violence was openly displayed for the greatest possible impact.

Two sets of organizations were crucial to the execution of Pinochet's approach to LSSR—comprising an essential component to the repressive cohort. On the one hand, there were Chilean-based death squads which committed a series of executions against political opponents of the government. On the other hand, introducing a factor that was not explicitly considered in an empirical investigation of the earlier chapter, there were US-assisted programs which provided intelligence, training, detention, and killing. Most notoriously, this included Operation Condor, which was a US-guided campaign of government-facilitated terror by South American dictators from Chile, Argentina, Bolivia, Paraguay, and Uruguay. During the 1970s and early 1980s these actors joined together in their desire to systematically eliminate leftist opponents and prevent the spread of Marxist ideology throughout the region. Under these efforts, the Chilean government classified and targeted dissidents and leftists, union and peasant leaders, priests and nuns, intellectuals, students and teachers. The cooperation and interaction worked at three levels: sharing intelligence, detaining and disappearing dissidents, and forming teams of assassins to take out political-opposition leaders and citizens. Operation Condor 2 extended this repressive strategy to targeted abductions, interrogations, and transfers of persons across borders (an example of what is now referred to as "transnational" repression). All told, during the dictatorship, more than 3,000 people were killed or disappeared but, as always, this should be treated as a conservative estimate.

Throughout the 1980s, many deaths originating from this earlier political motivation continued. Kidnappings and killings by private and paramilitary groups affiliated with government persisted. Terrorist acts against leftist civilians were thought to be supported by military organizations working on behalf of the regime. Military courts increasingly charged journalists for writing pieces that could be construed as oppositional. Judicial investigations of police torture were rarely undertaken because security force actors had no incentives to comply with the legal system's proceedings.

Individuals and organizations within civil society did not just sit quietly. Armed opposition during this time was limited to remote locales in the countryside (i.e., the Movimiento de Izquierda Revolucionaria) but protests took place in some of the more important parts of the country with an increasing presence. For example, what started as rather focused resistance from the Confederation of Copper Workers and National Workers Command progressively expanded to more routinized challenging behavior involving a diverse array of actors (e.g., the Catholic church, communist party, and ordinary citizens). These activities were met with increased levels of violence as the government actors shifted from the police to the military.

Interestingly, while our juggernaut theoretical argument finds support within this case there are nuances that our earlier discussion did not fully appreciate. Seemingly from the beginning of Pinochet's rise to power, there was some resistance within the predominate cohort which would later play important roles. For example, generals Gustavo Leigh (air force) and Arturo Yovane (a thirty-plus-year veteran of the carabineros/national police) were both critical during the early part of the spell and, consequently, they were removed and replaced with individuals who were believed to be more unconditionally supportive of the relevant policies. It should be noted that neither of these individuals was killed—something that will be commonly seen in other cases. Rather, they were reappointed in the case of Leigh and forced to resign in the case of Yovane.

There was resistance to repression actually built into the coalition fully codified in law, which was not fully acknowledged within our theory. For example, the Declaration of Principles issued by political leadership in 1974 clearly identifies that this right is anti-authoritarian and anti-hierarchical in nature supporting personal freedom, equality before the law, and property rights. This right of resistance was also revealed in the Chacarillas speech of 1977 delivered by Pinochet to an audience in Santiago where the commitment to recovery (from Allende's errors) was discussed along with a transition from military rule and normalization to something closer to democracy. One could say that this was cheap talk but actual institutions such as the Council of State were coming into being (during 1976) in order to facilitate the transition phase. Many of these topics were further outlined and implemented in the constitution of 1980.

One can also look to early activities of the Catholic church that would move against the repressive cohort as it facilitated the creation of the Committee of Cooperation for Peace in Chile from 1973 to 1975. This sought to monitor as well as advocate for human rights. In 1976 the church created the Vicariate of Solidarity in order to give support and voice to the victims of state repression—collecting information, assisting victims spiritually, legally, and financially. This grew to become an important pillar in the anti-repressive campaign that would emerge. In the 1980s, these efforts combined with the "Days of National Protest" (facilitated by some workers but mostly ordinary citizens), which involved distinct activities in the morning, strikes during the day, and clashes at night. During 1985 there was another cathartic moment with the murder of three communists which many perceived to be completely illegitimate and unnecessary—further turning popular sentiment against the regime.

On October 5, 1988, a scheduled plebiscite occurred where it was decided that Pinochet would be removed from power in two years. While the plebiscite brought certain state violence (sustaining the spell further), it served as an important turning point auguring in a democratic government that would begin to curtail the institutionalized abuses of human rights that had persisted during the Pinochet LSSR. For example, during this year, the state of emergency and state of danger to the internal peace were lifted. A year later (in 1989), there was a general election which saw Pinochet and some of those connected with him largely remove themselves from not only consideration but also influence. This perturbance allowed Christian-Democrat Patricio Aylin to become President. Despite this political change and consistent with our juggernaut theory of repressive spells, policies regarding human rights violations did not immediately shift that much because although Pinochet and his cohort were officially out of office, Pinochet still held the position of commander-in-chief of the army (a position he held until 1998) and other members of the cohort were not completely removed from their roles. By 1993, however, there was another general election which brought into office Christian-Democrat Eduardo Frei Ruiz-Tagle, who focused largely on poverty reduction, health, and education. This represented a very different scenario from 1989 because over the intervening years the Christian-Democratic alliance acquired the majority of seats in the Chamber of Deputies as well as the Senate. In this context, the Pinochet-led cohort was isolated as well as removed from power and the LSSR associated with them came to an end.

7.2.2 Senegal, 1985–2003

Within Senegal, the repressive spell between 1985 and 2003 began in response to two distinct behavioral challenges as our juggernaut theory would suggest.

On the one hand, the government confronted a general threat from the population. In 1985, there was mass opposition to the rule of President Abdou Diouf who previously served as secretary-general of the ministry of defense, director of the cabinet of the ministry of foreign affairs, director of the cabinet of the president, secretary-general of the presidency, minister of planning and industry as well as prime minister—all under Leopold Sedar Senghor, the first president of Senegal from 1960 to 1980. Reacting to this challenge, diverse repressive activities emerged including the declaration of martial law and the dissolution of the formal coalition of challengers. Despite these actions, scattered protests continued. One was an especially important one that took place right before the 1988 elections, which Diouf won amidst widespread perceptions of unfair and fraudulent electoral behavior. Another fraudulent election in 1993 extended Diouf's rule for another two years with resistance again being put forward. Most notably this included a string of student activism along with diverse labor organizations.

On the other hand, much of Senegal's repressive spell was associated with the separatist movement in the southern region of the country that took place during the 1980s. In opposition to the Muslim-majority central Senegalese country, Casamance peoples (dominated by the Jola group located in the southern part of the country) formed the Movement of Democratic Forces of Casamance (MDFC). Responding to this specific challenge, security forces and the police brutally sought out those involved. The police (in particular) were known to be incredibly violent and this activity was generally accepted from those in authority. Consistently, the government was unwilling to prosecute security forces for any human rights abuses that were identified and they often characterized challenging tactics employed during this period as "separatist riots" which were generally met with detention and torture.

In 2000, Abdoulaye Wade came to power after several earlier failures (hindered amidst claims of electoral fraud and his arrest for possible involvement in contentious activities at the time). This electoral shift took place amidst popular dissatisfaction with economic underdevelopment, a stranglehold maintained by political elites, a coalition of resistance being led by students as well as the unification of diverse political challengers. The change in leadership was believed to initiate a reduction in repressive activity but it actually continued the spell. Our juggernaut theory becomes useful here because it would lead us to seek out both similarities as well as differences between administrations. Such pursuit is useful because, although allowing for more political opposition than his predecessors, Wade's new constitution curtailed the right to hold protests, which clearly signaled a notable shift in the government's position. As a consequence of this continuity, there were limits to the rights of prisoners, women's rights were violated, detention as well as prosecution of journalists was commonplace and although arbitrary detention was disallowed, preventive detention was. In line with our argument, part of the continuity in behavior could be explained by Wade's pedigree. While seemingly distinct from Senghor and Diouf, he was indeed connected to them. Senghor allowed Wade to create his political party in the first place and Wade served as a member of the national assembly from 1978 to 1980 before being arrested for participating in protests about regarding one of Diouf's electoral victories. This insider-outsider dynamic continued for the next decade or so before he came to power.

Sixteen years after the spell's initiation (in 2001), however, two peace agreements were concluded with both sides attempting to end conflict and violence as well as restoring political normalcy to the besieged nation. State violence was minimized after these measures, but some forms of repressive behavior persisted in the years that followed. Again, we see that spells do not end immediately. With the primary reason for large-scale severe repression removed, the spell limped along for a few years until it finally ended in 2003.

7.2.3 Albania, 1976–2007

In many respects the dynamics involved with the Albania case are quite comparable to those identified above but in other ways the case is very different. The spell begins in 1976 under the authoritarian rule of Enver Hoxha—a devout Marxist-Leninist who adhered to the most orthodox version of the ideology despite reforms of his main allies in the USSR and China. Similar to earlier cases, by 1976, the Hoxha cohort had already been in power for several decades. Albania eventually turns away from its allies (viewing them as "traitors" to the socialist cause) and they attempt to "go it alone". Employing the Sigurimi security force agency as a main perpetrator, Hoxha guided a repressive campaign against all that challenged his rule. This included significantly restricting political and civil liberties (including religion as Albania was the first atheist state) and sending challengers to special facilities to house political prisoners (at one point there were 6 different institutions) as well as labor camps (at one point there were 14). Unlike the other repressive spells noted above, these activities did not respond to nor prompt mass resistance—at least not at this point.

By 1983, Albania was still in an LSSR spell but the repressive tactics themselves underwent some changes. On the one hand, in this year a decree was announced that allowed for the release of: people imprisoned for up to 8 years because of prior anti-state agitation, people arrested for crossing the border, and people in prison for political offenses who had less than a year left on their sentence. On the other hand, throughout 1983 and 1984, the Hoxha cohort investigated the minister of the interior and others that were suspected of plotting against the government. With this focus in mind, many were arrested and some were executed.

In 1986, Hoxha died and was followed by Ramiz Alia who, after an earlier heart attack, had been increasingly given more authority. While many were hopeful that this change in leadership might lead to a shift in policies in line with our juggernaut theory, Alia quickly vowed to continue ruling within the parameters established by his predecessor, which continued the repressive spell. This said, Alia continued Hoxha's repressive relaxation policy, pardoning: prisoners with sentences of up to 6 years for "anti-state agitation" or fleeing, female prisoners serving up to 20 years for political reasons, those with less than a year less on their sentence, and all prisoners under 18. Other political prisoners had sentences reduced by a one-quarter.

Relaxation of repressive behavior within the large-scale severe spell continued in 1990 when another pardon occurred including those aged over 60 and convicted of either anti-state agitation and propaganda or attempting to leave the country without permission, as well as those convicted of the same offences who had one year or less of their sentence left to serve. These pardons continued into 1991 despite some challenges emerging from the population as well as some counter-activities to control them. During this year, many demonstrations emerged—undertaken by individuals frustrated with the continued government restrictions and abuses. Interestingly and deviating from the period when Hoxha was alive, these activities led the government not to repress but to legalize opposition parties. Additionally, normally harsh restrictions on freedom of expression, conscience, and movement were also softened. People were given the right to passports and travel. Prison sentences for anti-state agitation were reduced to 10 years. People were given access to lawyers in legal situations and most prisoners in jail for religious reasons were released. In addition to this, the number of offenses punishable by death was reduced from 34 to 11, and women became completely exempt from receiving the death penalty.

By 1992, all Albanian political prisoners had been released. These occurred just as multi-party elections took place, the Socialist Party took power but with the first non-communist head of state. Due to widespread unrest, this government resigned soon after its victory. The following year, democratic elections placed Sali Berisha in power. Note that the country was still in a spell during this time and significant amounts of state repressive behavior were still being employed in part to address the instability of the (brief) transition as well as to establish/solidify Berisha's hold on power.

Although the number of offenses punishable by death was decreased, all laws of the communist dictatorship were replaced and new institutions were created. In 1994, those arrested under the category of "prisoners of conscience" increased as critics in the media but protesters were rounded up. During this time, it was common for anti-government protests to result in abusive police practices, and some people died from those activities.

As the spell continued, the next 8 years were quite volatile in terms of human rights violations. In 1996, some progress was made when the death penalty was entirely removed in times of peace, and crimes against humanity committed under communist rule were investigated. Regardless of these changes, legitimacy of the government was significantly reduced by a government-facilitated pyramid scheme that led to widespread protest. These efforts were not harshly repressed however and, in fact, the dissatisfaction of the population found its way into mainstream political mobilization. In 1997, although the democratic party won an election, it was broadly accused of election fraud (again) and there was seemingly no change in the repressive cohort or state behavior. The following year (1998) saw a lot of unrest in the country. In part, this was a reaction to the recent electoral malfeasance and mass disappointment with the outcome. The mobilization of this period was directed toward Berisha resigning but he would not relinquish power, resulting in a multinational force to step in and prompting early elections. The outcome of this contest was the victory of Socialist Rexhep Meidani—an academic with prior appointments to an electoral commission and the Albanian Center of Human Rights. Despite this partial shift in leadership, as Berisha was still a prominent figure in the political scene, the repressive spell still continued up until 2002 at which point it ended.

7.2.4 South Korea, 1980–96

According to our data, the repressive spell in South Korea lasted from 1980 to 1996. While the spell starts in 1980, the reason reaches back a bit further.

In 1948, Syngman Rhee became the first president of the Republic of Korea, following transfer from the US in the wake of World War II. Rhee's control over the relevant territory was always considered somewhat shaky and this resulted in a certain degree of violent heavy-handedness as well as corruption. By 1960, these behaviors became unacceptable to large amounts of the population and in April of 1960 mass protest arose. The response to this activity was repressed (which was consistent with what had come before) but the magnitude and severity of the government response appeared unacceptable to security forces who assumed power with Park Chung-Hee at the helm. While initially viewed in positive terms (especially compared to the earlier historical period), opinion began to sour toward Chung-Hee who barely won an open electoral contest in 1971. This led to his attempt to consolidate power with minor levels of repressive behavior. President Chung-Hee's efforts resulted in protest behavior as well as several assassination attempts before he was eventually assassinated in 1979 by the Korean Central Intelligence Agency. In the wake of this successful removal from power, security force agents pushed to consolidate another junta under the leadership of Chun Doo-Hwan and the LSSR of interest to our study was initiated.

Yet again revealing that repression can just as well suppress as it can incite, an anti-martial law demonstration occurred at Seoul Station on May 15, 1980, with nearly 100,000 students and citizens participating. In response to this, the government again ramped up repressive behavior even further. During this time, political opponents were arrested for dissident behavior, subject to beatings and other abuse in order to obtain confessions while in custody. Also at this point, the death penalty was widely being used and people were being arrested for things such as a connection to pro-communist groups.

By 1981, the constitution changed but Doo-Hwan maintained effective control over the government. This document promised to limit presidential terms as well as enhance freedom from torture, freedom of speech, press, assembly, and exclusion of forced confessions as court evidence. These things could be restricted however in the name of national security. In terms of repressive behavior, martial law was lifted and some presidential amnesties were granted but, reflecting the overall stickiness, human rights violations and the spell persisted. Similar to the earlier period, the National Security Law had some people arrested for connections to pro-communist groups and challengers faced the death sentence for leading anti-government organizations. In short, the general response was one of repression wherein young people were detained without warrants, journalists faced arrests for their work, and prisoners were ill-treated.

Despite the granting of presidential amnesties in both 1984 and 1985 as well as reports of limited torture in prison through the early 1980s, things generally persisted in this manner. In 1984, however, the number of offenses punishable by the death sentence increased. Sending a strong signal to the mass public, many political and religious personalities were placed under house arrest. Additionally, despite continued resistance, the government's coercive and forceful behavior persisted. For example, in 1986, 60 leaders of university student councils were arrested and accused of aiding North Korea through their professed belief in the liberation of the masses, democracy, and unification.

In 1987, another new constitution reinforced freedom of expression and association, safeguards against torture, and the right to access to lawyers for detainees, as well as habeas corpus rights. Almost immediately, fewer instances of torture took place in prisons. However, by 1988 people were still being arrested in large numbers for striking thousands of times in order to demand wage increases. Following the historical practice, strikers were accused of being pro-communist agitators which facilitated repressive action. Interestingly, although Doo-Hwan was removed from office, he essentially influenced the selection of his successors thereby maintaining a foothold in the "new" government under Roh Tae-Wood. This was not received well by the population that wanted the government to more fully open up and the June Democracy movement was born—a nationwide, largely peaceful protest that went on for a month before some concessions were offered by the government including a more open electoral process. Despite the new leader, therefore, the basic cohort influence still remained the same and the spell was continued.

By the early 1990s, torture in prison rose once again with many people dying. Prisoners of conscience were arrested frequently. During this time, police brutality on the streets was also a huge issue.

In line with our juggernaut theory, slowly things began to change. Regarding the importance of judicial aspects of democracy, small progress was made when the Public Security Law was repealed. Similarly, the National Security Law was amended to allow people to have connection with communist countries. The exception to this was North Korea. During 1993, Kim Young Sam, a former long-time opponent of the regime, came to power as the first freely elected civilian president. As expected by our theory, Sam engaged in numerous efforts to distance himself from the old regime. He arrested the two presidents before him for their part in coups and corruption. He granted amnesties to thousands of political prisoners and freed those involved with pro-democracy protests. Even with these activities, however, it still took three years for the spell to end. LSSRs can come to an end but it is clear that these terminations do not immediately follow electoral shifts.

7.3 Spell Sequence II: Start Spell, Civil Resistance, End Spell

Deviating somewhat from our theoretical argument, some of the spells in our database appear associated with civil resistance but not democratization. While broadly consistent with our theory, there is no institutional cohort destabilization.

7.3.1 Zambia, 1976–93

Within our data, Zambia's repressive spell lasted from 1976 to 1993. Similar to other cases, the president during much of this period (Kenneth Kaunda) and his United National Independence Party (UNIP) actually came to power before 1976 defeating a rival faction led by Harry Nkumula (leading the Zambian African National Congress). In 1964, the country gained independence from the United Kingdom. After this event, employing a nationalist-socialist ideology called "Zambian Humanism," Kaunda and his supporters helped establish and maintain an authoritarian, one-party system through extensive central planning and government coercion/force. By 1976, therefore, the spell had effectively been in effect for a decade.

Again, we see threats as providing the justification for onset. Domestically, all opposition parties were suppressed and eventually banned except the UNIP (citing civil unrest as the reason). Internationally, a continuous state of emergency was declared on the basis of neighboring countries being in conflict and Zambian security being threatened (an international variant on the domestic theme). This legislation allowed the government to ban many civil and political freedoms (including freedom of thought, expression, and assembly) as well as punish with imprisonment anyone who criticized the government-generally and/or the president in particular. The emergency was not the only relevant legislation but it was the most prominent. Interestingly, while focused around the presidency, the capacity of the office to actually direct the society through coercion/force was limited.

In the late 1980s and 1990, threats emerged that directly challenged the state of emergency. An increase in the price of corn meal caused increased mobilization in the form of food riots, led by student demonstrators. During the course of the unrest, the crowds attacked government buildings, looted shops, and set fires. The police and paramilitary units were sent to quell the behavioral challenges and they did this with excessive amounts of force, leading to dozens of deaths and injuries. In response to all of the societal conflict, some members of the Zambian army attempted a coup, but the effort was defeated by other members of government and the leaders of the attempt were prosecuted. While this conflict raged, the broader society (comprised of an incredibly impoverished rural population and slightly better off urban population) was largely disengaged. Indeed, the only organization that existed with any potential for mobilization involved trade unions—mining in particular which maintained an especially strong influence within the economy. The unions engaged in diverse challenges to object to government mismanagement of the economy as well as the low wages, unemployment, and excessive food prices. The response of political authorities to this threat was to ban strikes and put forward laws that hindered union behavior as well as to abuse union protests/protestors when they engaged in collective action. This continued the spell.

Over time, the economy continued to worsen—the value of copper, food production, and investment decreased and government regulation appeared highly ineffective. This led to reliance upon international assistance from the IMF (mirroring earlier reliance upon international investors) as well as increased debt which (in 1987) led to Zambian withdrawal from IMF obligation. The activity here with the World Bank was actually used by the Kaunda cohort in an interesting way because the International Monetary Fund was used as a scapegoat for the failed economy—leading to protests but not against the government this time but the international government organization. At the same time, Zambia became somewhat politically isolated. Attempting to navigate an independent path, Zambia did not really adhere to either the Western or Eastern blocs—reducing much needed military assistance. In addition to this, Zambia supported nationalist movements in Rhodesia, South West Africa, Angola, and Mozambique. While the spell continued, dissent, riots as well as strikes persisted. This, in turn, led to a repressive response from the military, but as seen above this led to still more resistance. Kaunda and his associates doubled down as they blamed the protests on outside agitation and moved to repress further but what is seen in the aftermath of this exchange is the growth of Zambian civil society—led by students, trade unions, and the church. This is the coalition that would build over time.

In 1991, things shifted. Unable to curb criticism of the one-party regime (even within the party itself), during this year, the Zambian political system opened up to a national referendum on the issue of opening up more broadly. This opportunity combined with increased prices on important food stuffs leading to greater anti-government mobilization. This unrest prompted a failed coup but the potential threat was sufficient enough to prompt change. Eventually a new president was elected and a new political party rose to prominence, displacing many of the cohort associated with the LSSR noted above. While this change decreased much of the violence and repressive acts in the country, some human rights abuses persisted in the years that followed (continuing the spell)—repression once again reveals itself to be quite sticky. Among the relevant behavior during this part of the spell, excessively long detentions, torture, and excessive force used during interrogations were common. Party militants, called vigilantes, assisted the police in engaging in these activities. The reason for the continuity was clear: the party and state became powerfully interwoven but essentially isolated from others. Gradually, however, with the decay of Kaunda's cohort and the behavior that they were trying to counter, the repressive spell finally came to an end.

7.3.2 Poland, 1976–87

The beginning of the spell in Poland in 1976 was marked by the presence of the largest working class uprising in a socialist government up to that time. Again, the explanation for the spell appears to predate the spell itself. Immediately following World War II, communism was introduced in Poland along with extensive repressive behavior directed by Stalinist policy. This begins to change following Stalin's death in 1953 as repressive behavior and economic decline ignited broader resistance as well as some shifts within the ruling party. For example, these brought into power Wladyslaw Gomulka—a long-time political operative who assisted with Polish national liberation, reconstitution after World War II and then rose through the ranks of the political establishment. Gomulka initially promised but later withdrew political reforms and prosecutions of those involved with earlier repressive behavior.[59] Despite extensive use of coercion and force, the Catholic church emerged as a strong presence in Polish civil society in the mid-1960s. By 1970, there was another wave of protest regarding economic difficulties, and guided by Gomulka as well as his associates numerous workers were killed. In the wake of this violence, Gomulka was replaced with his emerging political rival and USSR-favored (Edward Gierek). Gierek represented something of a shift to a younger cohort as the group of communists that arose prewar (like Gomulka) were aging. In this context, we get to the spell initiated in 1976—complete with mass protests and strikes regarding the economic decline/failure.

In response to the unrest and largely similar strategies employed under Gomulka, the Polish military and specific security forces within programs like Operation Summer 76 confronted, killed and dispersed crowds with tanks and helicopters. These efforts were largely effective—so much so that they compelled challengers (e.g., church groups, intellectuals, students, and workers) to go underground. This turned out to be important because the groups noted above joined together as they hid from the more overt manifestations of government coercion/force. Despite the success in prompting a behavioral retreat, however, the repressive spell was maintained.

Though the Gierek cohort survived the immediate threat, they were confronted with a rift that emerged within his support base—with one faction being led by Gierek's supporters including Eduard Babuich (Polish council of state chairman) as well as Piotr Jaroszewicz (deputy prime minister) and the other faction advocating for his removal led by Stanislaw Kania (another party member who somewhat rapidly moved up the ranks) and Wojciech Jaruzelski (a long-term military officer that had served in a variety of positions dating back to Gomulka who he helped remove from office).

In the context of the covert as well as occasionally overt struggle against the government, by 1980 essentially every sector of Polish society became involved. Some have suggested that approximately one-third of Poland's

[59] Repression was lower than it was before but there was still some level of application.

population participated in protest around this time. To counter these efforts, Solidarity was officially acknowledged as well as the right for workers to protest. Very important, at this point Gierek was removed from office as well as replaced with Kania and Jaruzelski dutifully declared martial law (in 1981). This further intensified the repressive behavior being carried out by the regime. Indeed, the policy augured in the most extensive internal military operation in the region. Within its wake, borders were sealed, a national curfew was imposed, and tens of thousands of activists (including Solidarity's leaders) were detained as well as abused. The regime made threats and government security forces carried them out, using excessive force and shooting into nonviolent crowds causing death and injury of protestors. During this time, Kania was removed and Jaruzelski emerged at the forefront of the cohort, the first military leader to assume control of a communist country. Regardless of this shift, however, anti-government street demonstrations (organized by Solidarity) continued into 1982 and beyond.

While many repressive spells are associated with a single authoritarian leader, Poland's case is one of political change and massive unrest that outlived the tenures of individual political leaders. During this time, security forces, like the Military Council for National Salvation, Zomos, and the citizen militia continually engaged in extensive repressive behavior. The goal of ending unrest came at a high cost to human rights, including previously held civil and political liberties. Demonstrations, occupations, and strikes of the period were combated by the government with tear gas, armored cars, water cannons, clubs, and light arms. Some demonstrators were attacked by multiple police officers, beaten into the ground, and left for dead. Additionally, physical abuse during interrogation of arrested demonstrators was very common. Part of the explanation for the excessive deaths can be attributed to the widespread distrust of institutions that prevented many injured people from going to the hospital, where they feared arrest and torture. This situation further increased the damage done as victims of repression did not receive much needed care. While individuals and groups were being brutalized in the street, various abuses were also taking place within prisons where tens of thousands of actual and suspected Solidarity members were held. Rather than docility however the high concentration of political activists in custody led to prison protests and hunger strikes.[60]

---

[60] Interestingly, despite the brutality of the time, much of the spell did not receive widespread attention. Indeed, the gravest abuses of the government were not widely known because of the government's secrecy and its suppression of the media as well as human rights groups.

Again, we see that the immediate impact of repression in one place/venue is greater contestation in yet a different place/venue.

Later in 1983, there was an important shift in government behavior. Although the end of martial law seemed like it would have ended the worst of Poland's repressive spell, Emergency Power legislation institutionalized many of the human rights violations in the country—keeping them alive several years longer. Freedoms of speech and the press stayed heavily restricted and journalists in particular as well as the media more generally were heavily suppressed. Assembly was also banned and protests disallowed.

Interesting, Jaruzelski resigns as prime minister in 1985 and Defense Minister in 1983 but he and those connected with him do not disappear from public life. Rather, Jaruzelski effectively becomes head of state with political affiliates taking over remaining positions. The repressive spell ends in 1987 but two years later, there were even greater political openings occurring with the restructuring of the presidency and increasing power being given to legislatures.

7.3.3   Madagascar, 1988–93

In 1988, a spell in Madagascar was initiated. At the time of the spell, leadership was held by Admiral Didier Ratsiraka who seized power in 1975 (a year before our dataset begins). As above, to understand the spell one needs to go back a little.

Upon consideration it is fairly clear that Ratsiraka was connected with a cohort that stretched back to the founding of the country. Initially, there was the leadership of Philibert Tsiranana from 1959 to 1972. He was the conciliatory, pro-French, and moderate first president of Madagascar. Next, there was Major General Gabriel Ramanantsoa in 1972—a military careerist hand-picked by Tsiranana when his leadership was threatened by extensive protest, an inability to counter the revolutionary movement Antananarivo and following a referendum authorizing a 5-year military takeover. This was followed by Colonel Richard Ratsimandrava in 1975. He was head of the police and Minister of the Interior of Ramanantsoa's government as well as a key military leader in the Triranana removal who had blocked an arrangement that would have lead to co-leadership with Ratsiraka. Time in office was short-lived. This leader lasted six days in office before he was killed by unnamed assailants. Following this, we have leadership going to General Gilles Andriamahazo. He stepped in for a few months following

Ratsimandrava's assassination but seemed to have no support for extending his tenure which leads to Ratsiraka.

Ratsiraka was definitely part of the earlier cohort but represented something of a marginal figure that was not really trusted by any side. There clearly was some history. He had served as Minister of Foreign Affairs under Ramanantsoa and before that as a military attache in France under Tsiranana. It is clear that he was favorably viewed by the security apparatus and it is also clear that a broad coalition of students, intellectuals, peasants, and middle class supported his leadership (under Zatovo Western Andevo Malagasy or ZWAM). This group arose to protest the ineffective responses of prior governments regarding a declining economic situation that seemed to privilege French interests over those of residents. Additionally, there seemed to be a strong desire to find someone who could forge a decent coalition across the political spectrum (something that others did not appear to be able or willing to do).

By most accounts, life under Ratsiraka's leadership did not end up being what it was hoped that it would be. He initially attempted to address prior economic failures by more wholeheartedly following the referendum-approved move toward socialism (discussed in the Charter of the Malagasy Socialist Revolution). Accordingly, Ratsiraka reached out to other socialist countries (on the continent and in Europe) and attempted to follow the path of the non-aligned movement. But, after a few years of not seeing any improvement (e.g., the perceived continuing favor being shown to foreigners over residents, business closings, and mass firings), he began to follow the advice of the IMF/World Bank as well as France, moving in a different direction. Specifically, his administration began to rely upon external funding as well as institutionalizing diverse lower-level repressive policies. Additionally, the military (a historical supporter of the Madagascar post-independence presidency) had been repeatedly targeted for plotting against the presidency. As a consequence, challenges began to emerge from both outside as well as within.[61] In 1982, Ratsiraka won re-election and repressive practices were extended further including a violent incident directed against "Kung-Fu" clubs which were not generally viewed well by the population.

---

[61] Clearly some of these were imagined but some revealed themselves to be quite real.

Despite some repressive action, the spell was not initiated until 1988 in the lead-up to the election of 1989. At this time, a group called the "Armed Forces" rose in opposition to Ratsiraka, his leadership and against the perceived corruption as well as inefficiency of the political-economy. This movement was (again) comprised of a broad swath of Madagascar civil society: e.g., political parties, church groups, workers' syndicates, farmers, and private sector groups. In response to the challenge, the government ramped up its coercive/forceful activities. Public gatherings were banned, violence was commonly used to break up demonstrations, and arrests were frequently employed but only against those engaged in overt challenges. As if state sponsored violence on the street and incarceration were not enough, rampant abuses existed in jail as well (e.g., starvation, untreated infections, and incredibly long sentences for political opponents).

In 1989, Ratsiraka (again) won an election but many perceived this contest to be unfree and unfair. As a consequence of the perceived impropriety, protests emerged calling for Ratsiraka to step down as well as for there to be a legitimate selection of the next political leader. Several of the challenges were quite noteworthy. For example, in 1990 there was an attempted coup which involved commandeering a national radio station. In the repressive response to counter this threat, however, a few individuals were killed and this led to popular perceptions of government overkill. Several of these challenges were quite large. On August 10, 1991, at least 400,000 people marched to the presidential palace, and regime-backed actors attacked the demonstrators with gunfire and grenades. In addition to the military-like response to counter relevant activities, the internal security forces (including urban and rural police) used stun grenades and tear gas—manifesting the heavy-handedness of the earlier era. Revealing a now common theme, the repression of the period did not work. Led by a coalition of opposition groups who sought an end to Ratsiraka's 16-year rule, the summer of 1991 brought daily mass protests under the large coalition entitled "Vital" or "Living Forces" (comprised of 16 different opposition groups); this was eventually led by Dr. Albert Zafy—a professor, a surgeon, and leader of a small political party.

Now, it should be clear that not all responses during the Ratsiraka-led spell were repressive—indeed, his alternating and occasionally simultane- ous repression and accommodating approach was one of his signatures. For example, at one point the civil service began striking (which crippled the administrative functioning of the government). After repressing some efforts, in part to address and channel threatening behavior, it was later announced that opposition parties would be allowed greater freedom. In May of 1991, the government offered 50 amendments to the constitution to address grievances; of course, the devil was in the details of the actual implementation but the effort assuaged some criticism and mobilization. And, in July of 1991, Ratsiraka yielded to popular demands—agreeing to dismiss his cabinet and appoint some individuals that were not his supporters/cohort members.

Moving into 1992, behavioral challenges expanded. True to form, the government responded to this challenge with yet more repression. Cracking down on peaceful protestors, the government responded with arresting opposition leaders, banning public gatherings, and using violence. If jailed, repressive action would continue as the imprisoned often faced starvation and deprived care leading to additional medical problems like infection, malaria, and tuberculosis. If imprisoned, persons may be held on extended sentences with no opportunity for release, even if found not guilty. Again, as we have seen numerous times above, the repression did not quell resistance. Indeed, the opposition continued and Ratsiraka's government declared a state of emergency which allowed further restrictions on public gatherings, censorship of the press and movement via a curfew.

By 1993, Ratsiraka was replaced with Albert Zafy as president and the spell came to an end. In line with our argument, one of the strongest selling points for Zafy as a leader was that he was believed to have no connection to Ratsiraka and the cohort that he emerged with. Interestingly, this turns out to not be completely true. Zafy had a connection to General Gabriel Ramanantsoa serving as Minister of Public Health and Social Affairs but after Ratsimandrava's ascension to power, he resigned and pulled out of mainstream politics as well as the cohort that was committed to state repression.[62]

---

[62] Interestingly, Ratsiraka is not completely removed from politics. Following his defeat, he returns to electoral victory but without repressive behavior being enacted. Another spell is initiated in 2002 when a new political leader, Marc Ravalomanana, comes to power. Ravalomanana represents something of a newcomer into national politics with a background not in the military but business and later local politics.

7.4 Spell Sequence III: Start Spell, Civil Conflict, Democratization/Civil Resistance, End Spell

7.4.1 Mali

Observing our data, there were cases which were even more complex than our juggernaut theory would suggest because several of the elements we highlighted above occurred at the same time. One such case involves two spells in Mali. Each is discussed below.

In 1977, a spell begins in Mali following the death of former president Modibo Keita (the country's first president and someone intricately connected with gaining independence from France). Keita had been placed in jail following a coup in 1968 led by General Moussa Traoré, Tiécoro Bagayoko, Kissima Doukara, Youssouf Traoré and Filifing Sissoko—known later as the Military Committee for National Liberation (MCNL). As often was the case, differences over how to address the economic situation served as the principal point of dissatisfaction. In addition, there was a strong anti-socialist critique that was tied to the strong-handed but restrictive (not especially violent) control over the government. This resulted in a decision to engage in a military takeover.

After Keita's death, the MCNL promised but failed to deliver an open political contest. This led to two challenges against the Traoré cohort auguring in the initiation of the LSSR. On the one hand, students and civil servants came together in protest to request Traoré's resignation on the grounds that the regime should be opened for contestation (as promised). This behavioral challenge was countered repressively as arbitrary arrests and harsh restrictions on speech and assembly were immediately applied. On the other hand, diverse plots were allegedly advanced which were suppressed as quickly as they were being announced. Indeed, until 1982 suppression of military rebellions was more or less constant as well as harsh. During this time, many in the security forces were arrested, tortured, and some were executed for their alleged involvement in the challenges being identified. In 1984, this first spell ends. Differing from our theory and many of the other cases discussed above, this termination is not associated with any shift in the general cohort but with an elimination of viable challenges.

The second spell begins in 1990. By this time, Traoré's cohort had a significant hold on a popularly perceived corrupt political-economy. This facilitated the development of both coherence around the policy of repressive action as well as mass resentment regarding the exploitative practices that emerged. Indeed, regarding the latter, it was generally known that those close to Traoré (proche de Moussa) did quite well. Colonial economic relations were exploited and international aid were directly siphoned off for the enrichment of this group and all exchanges were protected with coercion/force. This led to many enemies and one can readily see the impact by identifying who was protesting as well as the development of a competing coalition/cohort including the National Committee for Democratic Revival, Students Association of Mali and Democratic Alliance of Mali.

For example, in December of 1990, a series of protests emerge involving approximately 10,000 participants who were upset about licensing that hindered civilian ability to survive in the market which favored already established and larger companies tied to Traoré. This dissent was followed by another wave of protests involving approximately 30,0000 who broadly sought some form of political change. A third wave expanded the range of actors (e.g., clerics who pushed for a political opening). In response to each of these waves, the government engaged in extensive beatings and arrests as well as numerous threats about what would happen if behavioral challenges continued. This pattern of protest, expanding numbers of participants and increasingly violent repressive action continued throughout the spell.

After an especially violent series of exchanges, which involved a peak of approximately 100,000 protestors on March 4 of 1990 along with government agents shooting indiscriminately as well as lobbing grenades into crowds, on March 25, members of the security forces including members of his personal guard (Amadou Toumani Touré) arrested Traoré. Immediately following this event, members of the Traoré cohort were targeted for violence which (interestingly) kept the spell underway. Eventually, Traoré was tried and free elections were held in 1992, resulting in the election of Alpha Oumar Konaré. Despite the election, however, it took another three years for the spell to end. Again, although Konaré did have political ties to Traoré, serving as secretary-general in the party of President Keita in 1967, he did maintain a somewhat independent/outsider perspective as he worked with challenging institutions as well as occupied (and later resigned from) a ministerial position.

Why is this? Consistent with our argument, we would suggest that the slow termination of the spell was attributed to the political difficulties regarding the Tuareg—an ethnic group found in the North of the country. During the spell, Tuareg groups led rebellions throughout both Niger and Mali, aiming to achieve autonomy and form their own independent nation-state. The insurgency exacerbated an already difficult situation. Tuareg separatists attacked government buildings and their aggression led to a "full-blown rebellion" which inspired a response from the national army—among others. The rebels went against the state violently, using tactics both frequently as well as often broad in scope. The Malian soldiers were trained for regular combat and responded in ways which generated a large death toll. These activities did not however involve most of the population or large parts of Mali but they did sustain repressive behavior at a relatively large level. Indeed in 1991, the constitution was suspended and a state of emergency declared. Within this context, the military committed extrajudicial killings, and use of lethal force to put down demonstrations led to even higher death tolls and injuries. It should be noted that during this time, even peaceful demonstrations were met with lethal responses by security forces.

Into the early 1990s, the fighting/contention and democratization seemed to take a toll on the new government. In an effort to placate challengers, in 1991–2 the Malian government created a new self-governing region (the Kidal Region) and simultaneously provided the Tuareg with an opportunity for greater integration into Malian society. The Tamanrasset Accord Agreement on ceasing of hostilities (1991) would contribute to peacemaking, and the first democratically elected president Alpha Oumar Konaré was placed in to power in 1992. In 1995, moderates on both sides finally came together and the second spell came to an end.

7.4.2 Thailand

Perhaps the most complex case in our database involves Thailand which had three spells during the period of interest to our research. We will discuss two.

According to the data, the first spell began in 1976. The reason for this spell seemed straightforward enough: after nearly forty years of dictatorship involving Thanom Kittikhachorn, Narong Kittikhachorn, and Praphat Jarusathien, the country was transitioning to a democratic government involving several segments of the population in favor (e.g., students, workers, farmers, and academics) as well as several against (e.g., right wing party members and the military). At the same time, it would be remiss to ignore the ongoing civil conflict at the same time with the armed Communist Party of Thailand (CPT) which fielded 6,000–7,000 soldiers as well as almost a million sympathizers at its zenith in the north-eastern, northern, and southern regions of the country. Although this conflict existed (similar to discussion of the Tuareg of Mali), the actors and actions were largely disengaged from state-confrontations and the area functioned more in line with the idea of "dual-sovereignty" discussed by Charles Tilly as they were essentially a state onto itself within the larger nation-state. Threats also existed outside of the country as the CPT threat was connected to the broader international context with communist military victories taking place in neighboring Cambodia, South Vietnam, and Laos. Military mobilizations, small-scale attacks, refugees, and border crossings were constantly an issue.

Perhaps one the most memorable incidents within this early spell involved students. In October of 1976, 4,000–5000 unarmed youth had occupied Thammasat University where they engaged in diverse activities such as holding a mock re-enactment of an earlier dissident being hung. As criticism of the challengers grew, calls for a repressive response were finally answered as a brutal attack on students took place enacted by Thai state forces and far-right paramilitaries. Known as the "Thammasat University Massacre", this response involved killings, torture, hangings, and beatings. Following the event, a military coup occurred led by Admiral Sangad Chaloryu (inevitably putting into power conservative Thanin Kraivichien) and in response to the response civil conflict erupted throughout the country. During this period, many uprisings among students, peasants, and farmers emerged. Uniformly, all of these activities were met with state violence as the government tried to identify as well as neutralize all political rivals. The situation became so volatile that, perceiving an inability to stop the disruptions of order, a different faction of the military engaged in another coup in 1977, installing General Kriangsak Chomanand. Repression at the level of an LSSR was continued until 1986.

Interestingly, at the same time that the activities above were taking place, some conciliatory processes were also being introduced. For example, there was an amnesty given for those who engaged in the demonstrations at Thammasat University called the "Amnesty for Those Who Committed Wrongdoing in the Demonstrations at Thammasat University between 4 and 6 October 1976." This was passed by the national legislative assembly on September 15, 1978. Of course, this was preceded by an amnesty for those who engaged in the coup and something of a silent amnesty for those that engaged in the massacres. Two years later (in 1980), the Thai government offered an amnesty for those within the CPT to give up their arms and enter the political system as fully incorporated members. There were numerous reasons for this: increased divisions within the ruling party existed regarding the Sino-Soviet split, the Chinese invasion of Vietnam (very much seen as a betrayal of the communist cause), greater understanding of the incredibly violent and widely illegitimate activities of the Khmer Rouge in Cambodia (another communist cause), improved relations between the Chinese and Thai governments as well as lucrative offers of housing and security to reduce the likelihood of retribution. In 1982, a large number of the rebels laid down their arms effectively ending the threat—the reduction in support from China as well as the realization of what communist-affiliated Khmer Rouge had done also reduced support. The effective dissolution of the CPT was followed by a reduction in non-government and government violence overseen jointly by General Prem Tinsulanonda (the victor in yet another military takeover) and King Bhumibol Adulyadej whose presence as well as importance had varied overtime but nevertheless remained salient. Bolstered by diminished political threat as well as sustained economic growth (which reduced popular grievances), the spell ended in 1986.

Contention in Thailand was far from over. Responding to perceived inequities in the distribution of resources to military personnel in 1991, a different part of the military engaged in a coup calling itself the "National Peace Keeping Council." To provide some legitimacy to the effort, the junta put a civilian prime minister as its figurehead (Anand Panyarachun) but the military still maintained effective control of all things both political and miltiary in nature. While the target of the coup was the top of the political apparatus, repressive behavior was also enacted against the population— initiating another spell. As part of a normalization and democratization effort, a general election was held in March 1992 which led to the appoint- ment of a military leader as well as coup participant Suchinda Krapray- oon, which seemed to represent a return to military rule. Fearing the re- emergence of dictatorship, a variety of demonstrations took place, including some of the largest ever seen within the country. Similar to the earlier period, these activities were responded to brutally as Kraprayoon used units of the military directly tied to him to attack the challengers. Violent suppression of protests often involved beating or disappearing persons. In some cases, summary executions were enacted by police and security forces.

Many of these activities were legitimated publicly by the "destroy the enemy" order against pro-democracy demonstrators enacted by the govern- ment, which targeted all who engaged in peaceful assembly. The repressive spell involved regular beatings by police of prisoners, criminal suspects, and other detainees. Torture, like electric shock, was widely used to get information from the imprisoned to help identify who was involved with behavioral challenges. Faced with a potentially violent situation the likes of which had not been seen above, the king ended up re-intervening in politics as well as re-appointing Panyarachan to the prime minister position where he sat until 1992 when there was an election. While our argument would have led us to exclusively focus on civil society-which was central to the overall story, if we had stayed strictly within these parameters, we would have missed the key role played by the king in bringing about a change in government policy. Correct in the broad strokes, the particular pathway in this second spell would have been missed. Two years later, again revealing the stickiness of state repression, the spell was ended.

8

What We Can Do to Better Understand, Prevent, Reduce, and End Repressive Spells

8.1 Introduction

People the world over have had an interest in trying to deal with large-scale, severe repressive behavior (what we abbreviated to LSSR). This objective has existed since the very founding of the nation-state but it was not until the latter part of the twentieth century that governments and non-government actors had the interest as well as wherewithal to try and take this problem on in a systematic manner. It was years later that academics tried to evaluate some of the effectiveness of these efforts—admittedly in a limited fashion. Given the objective of preventing, reducing, and ending LSSR, the question has remained: what is the most effective way to achieve the desired end? Within this chapter, we seek to use our theoretical argument as well as the empirical results from our numerous analyses presented throughout the book to develop an anti-repressive research and policy agenda for answering the question posed above. This involves first reviewing our theory and the analysis of the repressive life cycle—highlighting what is statistically as well as substantively important. Equally as meaningful, this involves discussing what is statistically as well as substantively unimportant. All the while, we try to highlight what needs to be done so that the next 40 years worth of scholarship, advocacy, mobilization and funding may be better than the last.

8.2 Repression 2.0

The argument we advance in this book (the juggernaut theory of repressive spells) rests upon a fundamental reconceptualization of repressive behavior away from thinking about isolated events (rates) and categories (levels)

The Death and Life of State Repression: Understanding Onset, Escalation, Termination, and Recurrence.
Christian Davenport and Benjamin J. Appel, Oxford University Press. © Oxford University Press 2022.
DOI: 10.1093/oso/9780197655375.003.0009

viewed at the nation-year.[63] Instead, we suggest that the appropriate unit of analysis to evaluate and understand is the repressive "life cycle" across onset, (de)escalation, termination, and recurrence. This follows the study of other forms of large-scale political conflict and violence such as interstate war, insurgency/counter-insurgency (i.e., civil war), terrorism/counter-terrorism, revolution/counter-revolution, and protest/protest policing. It makes sense to adopt such a perspective because detailed historical evaluations of the topic generally discuss the phenomenon in these terms. Additionally, it follows from the most stable but least theorized empirical finding in this literature: the positive impact of prior repressive behavior on subsequent activity. Rather than view this result as simply a control or as a nuisance to get rid of during estimation, we acknowledge that it actually contains useful information and that it prompts us to rethink the repressive process overall—viewing it as one where the past has important implications for the course of state repression. To be clear, we do not believe that governments are wholeheartedly subservient to this past, but we do believe that they are guided by it in extremely powerful ways and that in order to impact state repressive behavior, one must evaluate it with this influence in mind.

Deviating from existing research, within this book we suggested that the repressive process is better thought of as being partially rational and more like a slow moving, momentum-generating juggernaut. We advance this position because we believe that political authorities engage in some kind of light cost-benefit analysis to determine when they will engage in repression but this is largely done only at the beginning of a spell. After this initial calculation and implementation, political authorities as well as security force agents lock into the decision to use force/violence avoiding serious revisitation of its logic as well as counter-arguments for other activities. Such a position necessitates the identification of factors that hinder the positive/favorable evaluation of repressive behavior before it is implemented and after it is underway the identification of factors that disturb the cohort that favored the selected repressive policy in the first place.

With these ideas in mind, we focused our effort on addressing government behavior that has historically proven to be the most impactful on human life—state-sponsored activities that are violent and large-scale in the scope of their targeting. The behavior here has gone by many names—genocide, politicide, democide, state terror, state repression, human rights violation,

---

[63] By isolated we mean considered on their own.

atrocity, mass killing, one-sided violence—regardless, they all involve the same characteristic features regarding violence, scope, and perpetrators (political authorities).

To measure what we refer to as LSSR we use a modified version of the dataset known as the Political Terror Scale or PTS (Wood and Gibney 2010)—the most widely used global database on state repression.[64] Our conception is distinct from existing literature because we do not consider lower-levels of repressive behavior. We are not interested in understanding variation in repression. Instead, we use only the three highest values of this indicator: i.e., where behavior becomes violent as well as systematically applied to large amounts of the population. This is done because we would maintain that most citizens, activists, advocates, and governments have been and are interested in avoiding behavior that falls into this category and not the lower-level manifestations. With this conception, a repressive "spell" is initiated when PTS rises to 3 or above and it is sustained until it goes below this level. As conceived, this gives us approximately 250 spells between the years 1976 and 2006, which we view as an ideal laboratory to explore the topic as various repressive applications as well as strategies to impact this behavior existed at this time. Further differentiating our effort from prior research, we examine these data not at the nation-year but at different phases in the "repressive life cycle". This includes onset (i.e., the initiation of a spell), escalation (i.e., moving upwards in a spell once underway), termination (i.e., the end of a spell), and recurrence (i.e., the onset of a spell in a place that already had one).[65]

Representing one of the most comprehensive efforts yet undertaken, we consider a wide range of variables and policies that have been thought to influence state repression as well as implemented in order to influence LSSR for decades throughout the world-at an expense in the billions, if not trillions. This includes factors that emerge within nation-states (e.g., electoral as well as judical aspects of democracy, electoral democratization, civil war, domestically-sponsored civil resistance, economic development, population size and youth bulges); factors that emerge outside of nation-states (e.g., military intervention, economic sanctions, international law/human rights treaty ratification, IGO membership and preferential trade agreements); and

---

[64] We also use other measures to validate our selection and consider other measures to evaluate our arguments. As this reveals similar results, we just simplify the discussion to use PTS.

[65] As some of the dependent variables are slightly different they required different types of analyses but they are connected conceptually to the idea of different phases of a life cycle or spell.

domestic-international hybrids which combine the two (e.g., internationally-sponsored civil resistance as well as INGO presence).

To conduct the relevant analyses we use methods that are appropriate for the different aspects of the repressive cycle-explicitly drawing upon insights generated from the exploration of other forms of political conflict and violence.

What did we find? The results from our analyses are provided in the table below. We use these first to discuss a new policy agenda for those interested in stopping and reducing state repression and then to discuss a new research agenda directed toward the same ends.

8.3 Towards a New Policy Agenda

Viewing the results cumulatively in the table allows us to think about an anti-LSSR policy agenda in two different ways. First, we can think about what policy works across the largest number of phases (i.e., which variable/policy offers us the broadest range of humanitarian applications). Second, we can think about what policies work within the context of a specific phase (i.e., which variables/policies offer us a more narrow range of humanitarian applications). Neither topic has been explored within prior literature. These are addressed in the next two sections.

8.3.1 Across-Phase Influences

It seems clear from the table that the policy which reduces repression across the most phases of a spell involves electoral democratization. This policy shows up in three different phases as being statistically and substantively important in a direction that moves against LSSRs. Electoral democratization decreases the likelihood of onset, it increases the likelihood of termination, and it decreases the likelihood of recurrence. We explain this finding by the disturbance that this policy has on cohorts of political authorities and security force agents who cohere around policies of state repression/human rights violation. The implication here is clear: if one wanted to invest in one strategy to hinder/diminish/eliminate spells in some way, electoral democratization has the most powerful impact across categories! Interestingly, the one phase of the repressive spell that is not impacted by electoral

Table 8.1 Summary of Empirical Results

Ind. Variables	Onset	Escalation	Termination	Recurrence
Civil Conflict	+	+	−	ns
Economic Development	−	ns	ns	−
Population	+	+	−	+
Youth Bulge	ns	ns	−	ns
Civil Conflict Termination	ns	−	+	ns
Electoral Democracy	−	−	ns	ns
Electoral Democratization	−	ns	+	−
Judicial Democracy	ns	−	+	ns
Civil Resistance (Domestic)	ns	ns	ns	na
Civil Resistance (International)	ns	ns	ns	ns
INGO Presence	ns	ns	ns	ns
Human Rights Treaties	ns	ns	ns	ns
PTAs	−	ns	ns	ns
IGO Membership	ns	ns	+	ns
Economic Sanctions	ns	+	ns	ns
Pro-government Interventions	ns	+	ns	−
Anti-government Interventions	ns	ns	ns	ns
Neutral-government Interventions	+	+	ns	+
Time counter	ns	na	−	ns

Note: Results based on Full Model. + = positive and statistically significant, − = negative and statistically significant, ns = not significant. Significance based on .10 level.

democratization concerns escalation. Democratization offers no assistance if this is the objective being pursued.

Given the importance of electoral democratization to LSSR, it is also important to highlight specific options (considered within the book as domestic-international hybrids) where specific international forces impacted the likelihood of specific domestic behavior. For example, our results disclose that two policies have indirect effects on LSSRs via democratization. In three models (onset, termination, and recurrence), civil resistance and INGO involvement increase the likelihood that political systems move in the direction of democracy. This indirect path is incredibly important as one begins to think about what can/should be done about pacifying large-scale, severe repressive action.

Across two phases of the repressive life cycle, three policies emerge as being statistically as well as substantively important. First, relevant to the last variable (democratization), the level of electoral democracy is found to have an impact. This policy reduces the likelihood of onset as well as escalation once a spell is underway. Such a finding makes sense because these systems tend to increase the likelihood of some citizen participation/evaluation in selecting policymakers who would hopefully avoid activities like repression out of fear from being removed from office—all else equal. The level of judicial democracy is important as well. Specifically, this policy decreases the likelihood that spells escalate once underway. Such institutional arrangements are also connected with increasing the likelihood that spells come to an end. While the impact of electoral democracy is similar to judicial democracy, we maintain that the latter mechanism is different because independent courts serve as a much-needed check upon political authority which hinders repressive behavior. Courts may further provide information to citizens which helps them understand what political authorities are doing and what should be targeted with subsequent mobilization (similar to what Lani Guinier calls "Demos Prudence"). The last policy/variable concerns civil war termination. Specifically, we find that when these forms of political violence come to an end, LSSRs are less likely to escalate and they are more likely to terminate. Interestingly, civil war has no influence on LSSR onset or recurrence.

Now, individuals might find it puzzling that we highlight the importance of political democracy when researchers, policymakers, and activists have been increasingly debating the merits of such a policy. This is quite a heated debate actually with some questioning the extensive spending and effort that has been put into it and others extolling the many virtues of its application. Ours should be viewed as a focused contribution to this larger discussion highlighting one specific outcome—state repression. On this point, our results are unambiguously clear. If one wanted to do something about ending/reducing LSSR, then a major part of the answer involves democracy and (especially) movements towards it. Of course, we don't believe that democracy and democratization can do everything and here much of the debate is reasonable; rather, we believe that among the options generally discussed and which humans can have a hand in influencing in some manner, democracy and democratization are probably the best bet for preventing, limiting, and ending state-sponsored, large-scale, and violent repressive action.

8.3.2 Within-Phase Influences

An alternative way to think about building an anti-LSSR policy agenda is to think about what influences the different phases of the repressive life cycle—viewed individually. In addition to the negative influence of democracy and democratization on onset, when we consider what else hinders the initiation of spells, we find economic development plays a role. Specifically, within advanced economies we see a lower likelihood of LSSRs beginning. This serves as a clear policy option for those that wish to head off subsequent humanitarian crises that might be more unwieldy and expensive to impact once they are underway. Results disclose fairly straight-forward solutions for decreasing escalation which are generally consistent with what was highlighted in the discussion of across-phase influences (i.e., electoral democratization, judicial democracy, and civil war termination). LSSR termination is impacted by the same three variables but in addition to this we also find the importance of IGO membership. This policy is significant because it reveals that under certain circumstances international factors can have a direct and powerful pacifying influence on a phase of the repressive life cycle. Finally, we come to the topic of spell recurrence. From the results of our empirical investigation, we (again) see that electoral democratization and economic development reduce the likelihood of a spell returning. Interestingly, and somewhat surprisingly, we also find that pro-government intervention decreases the likelihood of a repressive recurrence. This policy appears to significantly increase the capacity of the repressive apparatus which likely reduces the threat perceived by the government and the perceived necessity for state repression/human rights violation to deal with it.

8.4 Towards a New Research Agenda

Viewing the results cumulatively allows us to think about what researchers should do moving forward.

First and foremost, our study has implications for the conceptualization of state repression/human rights violation. One could not leave our research without acknowledging that evaluations of nation-years (the predominant unit of analysis for approximately 50 years) is clearly an inappropriate way to think about the subject. Instead, we suggest that researchers focus on spells as the unit of analysis, along with the various phases of the life cycle that emerge from this approach including onset, (de)escalation, termination, and recurrence. Without addressing repressive behavior in this manner, one is likely to evaluate state coercion and forceful behavior out of context as well as with an inappropriate method of analysis. While such a conceptualization is now standard in related areas (i.e., interstate war, civil war, social movements, and civil resistance), it is novel in the area of state repression/human rights violation. This needs to change!

Second, our reconceptualization of the unit of analysis compels new theorization. In our work, we advocated and found support for our juggernaut theory of repressive spells where costs and benefits are evaluated initially but then these calculations become institutionalized into diverse policies and the activities associated with them. This has numerous implications for scholars of repressive behavior. For example, such an approach compels those interested to search for factors that hinder the process favoring state repression—in our work we maintain that the level of democracy and democratization plays this role. Accordingly, we would suggest that researchers should evaluate causal influences over time as the clock is literally ticking with weakening ability to influence the repressive process as momentum in the repressive process builds.

Third, our reconceptualization compels researchers to identify and analyze what we referred to as repressive "cohorts" (i.e., politicians and security force agents who come to decide that repression/human rights violation is the strategy that they wish to enact). Specifically, scholars interested in the topic should explore who is in them, how they are connected to one another, when they disagree as well as when they fall apart. This is very different from previous work which has largely ignored cohorts in particular and perpetrators in general. Recently, a few have paid attention to perpetrators but only a select number has paid attention to political authorities and hardly anyone has highlighted the political-economic elites who favor such policies. This is something discussed in early research on the topic of state repression on dependency but this work has been largely ignored by subsequent generations. A more detailed evaluation of cohorts is precisely where research needs to go.

Fourth, the findings in this book reveal that there are certain empirical results which appear to promote peace in terms of hindering LSSRs. If one wanted to promote such an option, these factors should be examined further. There are also some factors that appear to consistently promote state violence. If one wanted to promote peace, then these would need to be investigated in greater detail.

For example, there are three variables that seem to promote state repression across different phases: civil conflict (present in every phase except recurrence), population (always present and working against peace), and neutral government intervention (present in every phase except termination). All three are present within the context of onset as well as escalation. Two are present within the context of termination and two are present within the context of recurrence. If one was trying to develop a research agenda, these three factors should be prioritized. While civil war and population are not surprises in this category, clearly neutral government interaction would be as it is so commonly believed that these activities would serve as facilitating peace.

In addition to these three variables which we see across phases, there are a few variables that emerge when we consider phase-specific influences. For example, the likelihood of onset is increased by civil conflict, population, and neutral intervention—with no other variables being identified. Escalation is increased by the same three variables in addition to economic sanctions as well as pro-government interventions. The second variable (pro-government interventions) is not surprising as enhanced coercive capacity for the state would be associated with an increased likelihood of perceived effectiveness as well as decreased cost—factors that would increase government willingness to ramp up repressive behavior. The first variable (economic sanctions) is somewhat surprising however because these are supposed to hinder government coercion and violence. Instead we maintain that this activity further threatens political authorities and compels them to lock in to the policy that they believe might save them—LSSR.

Termination is hindered by conflict and population (again) but these are also joined by two other variables: youth bulges and time. The former had been identified in other research where it was believed that governments act pre-emptively to eliminate subsequent mobilization/behavioral challenges. Our research suggests that these concerns are relevant to authorities sustaining repressive behavior but not its onset or escalation. These variables are nearly impossible to impact in any way and therefore they are not especially useful for the development of anti-repressive policy but they are helpful for contextualizing what can be changed which is something that should be examined more consistently.

Related, time is found to be relevant in order to prolong LSSR spells because it is revealed that the longer they go on, the more likely they are to persist. This directly supports our argument about momentum and repressive juggernauts being incredibly difficult to disassemble once underway. Such a finding suggests that it is better to try and end spells earlier in their life cycle (prevention and early termination) rather than later. This is a point that has not explicitly been made before (based on empirical evidence) but it has been something consistently highlighted by human rights groups, activists and some international organizations. Indeed, if one looks back at the discussions about what to do about LSSRs over time, they can see an increasing but variable discussion regarding the prevention of mass killing, its termination and the punishment of those who perpetrated it. This is where we see our work contributing: we need to get back to prevention!

Fifth, our study ends in 2006 but it is an empirical question whether the results are temporally bound or if they extend up to the present. Clearly, the discussion of the topic persists. Governments, NGOs, advocates, activists, and ordinary citizens the world over are still trying to figure out what (if anything) works and what role democracy as well as democratization play. We considered what can be viewed as a unique period for our investigation. During the time period examined, the world saw numerous movements to democracy (i.e., the "third wave", post-USSR development and the "Color" revolutions) but also numerous movements away from it. We also saw a tremendous willingness to extend resources to deal with state repression/human rights violation. It is an empirical question whether distinct periods will reveal similar influences to those identified here but given the topic and the limited number of factors that appear to address the suggestions put forward by our juggernaut argument, it seems more than appropriate that researchers consider the topic both explicitly and extensively.

Finally, we would say something about the line of inquiry related to state repression, human rights violation, genocide, and one-sided violence. In many respects, "Never Again" has moved from a very particular phrase referencing the Holocaust to a phrase referencing a general call to consider/act against large-scale, severe repression broadly conceived. While well intentioned, however, much of this effort has resulted in individuals and organizations in as well as out of the academy focusing on a particular variable/policy or small set of variables/policies, regardless of actual impact (which is rarely [if ever] assessed). In a sense, there has been momentum and institutionalization developed with regard to responding to state repression which is also something worthy of rigorous examination—how humanitarian ideas and policies get fixed in government, NGO, academic, and popular imagination. Unfortunately, rather than "Never Again", such thinking and behavior has resulted in situations better characterized as "Ever Again". It is hoped that our research can assist in opening a conversation about the wisdom of such an approach as we seek a less violent world. A detailed history of all solutions that exist (not just the ones put forward), how one should/could gauge efforts, and an evaluation of how well the different solutions have done would go a long way to advancing this objective. We hope that our book facilitates such an effort by pointing out some of the factors involved with generating an appropriate response to the problem. Only in this context could we truly move toward answering the call to "Never Again" allow state sponsored violence to occur.

Robustness Checks

In this appendix, we estimate over 30 additional models across the four main response variables (onset, escalation, termination, and recurrence) to assess the robustness of the empirical results reported above. The models include: (1) alternative coding rules for LSSR, (2) alternative repression data, (3) a different survival estimator, and (4) methods to assess potential endogeneity concerns. Across the additional models, the results concerning democratic change (our main independent variable of interest) are generally consistent with the findings from the main text. From these analyses, we observe that democratic transitions are associated with a lower probability of LSSR onset and recurrence and higher probability of LSSR termination. These additional findings provide strong support for the theoretical argument advanced in the book.

A.1 Alternative Coding Rules

To start, we modify the coding rules for LSSR spell onset, escalation, termination, and recurrence to demonstrate that our findings are robust across different ways to operationalize and measure spells.

First, we re-estimate our models on the gravest spells, or those with PTS scores of only 4 or 5. Second, we drop spells that last only a single year. Both robustness checks directly speak to potential concerns about the magnitude of repression in our spells. That is, it is important to assess whether democratic transitions are still associated with the gravest spells. Dropping PTS scores of 3 allow us to select on the worst spells, while the data indicate that most spells that only last for one year are on average less severe than spells that persist for multiple years. Both tests allow us to focus on the worst case scenarios.

As one can see in Figures A.1 and A.2, the results mirror the findings from the main text—democratization is associated with LSSR onset, termination, and recurrence. At the same time, we find little support for the impact of democratization on LSSR escalation.

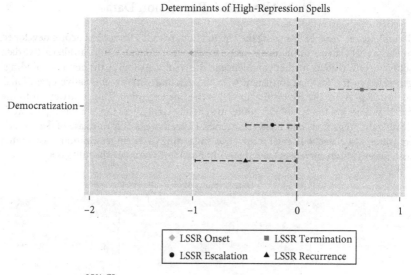

Fig. A.1 Determinants of LSSR, 1976–2006

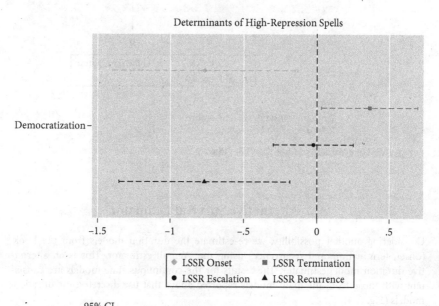

Fig. A.2 Determinants of LSSR, 1976–2006

A.2 Alternative Repression Data

Second, we re-create LSSRs using the Latent Human Rights Protection Scores developed by Fariss (2014) to use a different measure to test our argument. We use an alternative data source to give readers further confidence in the results. As found, the empirical findings generated in the text are consistent with those found with an alternative operationalization (Fig. A.3). The recurrence model is the one exception. This is attributed to the fact that there are too few observations to systematically assess the relationship between democratic transitions and LSSR recurrence. Here, there is only one case of democratic transition associated with spell recurrence, suggesting that democratization is associated with fewer LSSR recurrences even if it is not possible to estimate the full model.

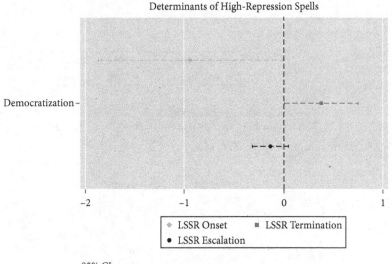

95% CI
Time and constant variables omitted.
Robust standard errors, clustered on country.

Fig. A.3 Determinants of LSSR, 1976–2006

A.3 Alternative Survival Estimator

Considering another possibility, we re-estimate the duration models from the book (onset, termination, and recurrence) using the Weibull estimator. This is an alternative duration model estimator. The results for the continuous-time models are consistent with those from the main models reported above that use discrete-time duration models (Fig. A.4).

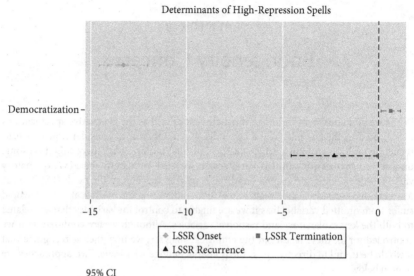

95% CI
Time and constant variables omitted.
Robust standard errors, clustered on country.

Fig. A.4 Determinants of LSSR, 1976–2006

APPENDIX B

Endogeneity Concerns

While we find consistent results in the main text as well as the alternative specifications investigated in the last part of the appendix, it is important to consider how concerns related to endogeneity impact the statistical results. In particular, there might be some unobserved factors (or omitted variables) associated with both the key explanatory variable—democratic transitions—and the response variables in the book (LSSR onset, termination, escalation, and recurrence). Put differently, the statistical results would suffer from omitted variable bias if we are unable to control for variables that are related to both the key explanatory and response variables. Although we are confident that we controlled for all these factors in the empirical analyses, we nonetheless recognize that it would be useful to directly assess the potential endogeneity issue. Two approaches are offered below.

First, we employ fixed effects to ensure that our results are robust to concerns related to omitted variable bias. As conceived, fixed effects account for unobserved factors that influence both the independent and dependent variables, thereby reducing omitted variable bias. In particular, the estimator controls for any unobserved factors that are constant over time but vary between governments/spells. Generally speaking, fixed effects models include a dummy variable for each unit that holds constant the unobserved differences across units (i.e., unmeasured differences between United States and Zimbabwe).[66] This is particularly useful because accounting for these differences eliminates the "cross-sectional" variation related to unobserved heterogeneity which is the most likely source of bias resulting from omitted variables in the present analysis.[67] As a result, we can estimate a model that satisfies the "ignorability assumption", allowing us to better assess the relationship between the independent and dependent variables.[68]

---

[66] Fixed effects models only deal with time-constant unobserved heterogeneity. This is likely a smaller limitation here due to the relatively small time-frame in the sample.

[67] By eliminating the cross-unit variation, the statistical results are based on the remaining variation, or within unit variation. In other words, fixed effects estimate the average effect for a variable within units over time.

[68] It is also important to note that nonlinear fixed effects have an important limitation in that it drops all units/panels with no variation on the dependent variable (i.e., all zeroes, for example). While this is a consequential shortcoming, fixed effects still provides a useful way to account for unobserved heterogeneity and the biases that result from it, while also providing for an important robustness check on the results.

Second, we employ instrumental variable (IV) regression to deal with unobserved variables that are related to democratization and the error term. In other words, we focus on the ignorability assumption as it relates to the democratization variable. We focus on democratization because our theory leads us to believe and empirical findings generally support that this type of variable should matter.[69]

To be considered a valid instrument IV regression requires that a variable meet two assumptions: (1) it needs to be correlated with democratization but (2) it needs to be uncorrelated with the error term in the primary model (and subsequently the relevant dependent variables) conditional on the independent variables. While recognizing how difficult it is to find a valid instrument, we employ rainfall shocks as an instrument in the IV regression models below.

Drawing on the extant literature, we argue that climate shocks lead to a window of opportunity for democratic transitions due to its negative impact on economic growth (e.g., Aidt and Leon 2016; Bruckner and Ciccone 2011). We operationalize climate shocks as the annual deviation in precipitation from the 10-year moving average at the country-year level (Salehyan and Hendrix 2014). Further, the instrument satisfies the two key assumptions. Existing literature finds that climate shocks are linked with democratic transitions, satisfying the strength of instrument criteria. At the same time, this variable meets the exclusion restriction assumption because we see no theoretical reason to believe that rainfall is correlated with the error term (and thus different aspects of a spell) except through the independent variables which satisfies this assumption.[70]

As discussed in detail below, the results from both the fixed effects and the IV regression models lend strong support to the validity of the main set of results including the primacy of domestic politics in explaining the different phases of LSSR. In the following sections, we detail the robustness checks for the different stages of LSSR.

B.1 LSSR Onset

B.1.1 Fixed Effects Regression

In Figure B.1, we employ the results from the nonlinear fixed effects regression. To estimate this, we use the same specification from the full model with all the control, domestic, and independent variables. The unit of analysis is the government-year. The dependent variable measures the onset of LSSR and equals 1 when and LSSR

---

[69] Furthermore, it is clear that democratization is a nonrandom process and that it is difficult to control for all factors related to it given disagreements in the literature about determinants (Gassebner, Lamla, and Vreeland 2013; Ulfelder 2010). In addition, while fixed effects allow us to deal with all time-constant and across-unit unobserved heterogeneity, IV regression focuses on the the unobserved factors that may bias the results on democratization.

[70] We assess the strength of the instrument using an F-test, in which the general rule of thumb is that the F-statistic should be greater than 10 (Staiger and Stock 1994). The F-statistic meets this condition for all three models, and thus satisfies this assumption. We unfortunately cannot assess the exclusion restriction assumption because a test that approximates it (i.e., Hanson J statistic) requires that the model be over-identified (i.e., more instruments than endogenous regressors). We, however, only have one instrument (rainfall) and therefore our model is not over-identified.

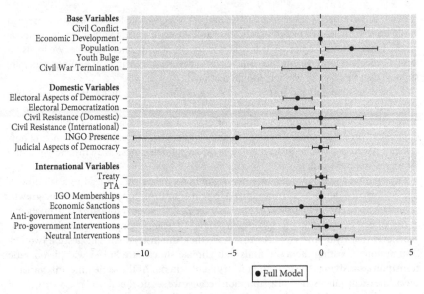

N=1,782. Constant omitted.
Robust standard errors, clustered on country.

Fig. B.1 Determinants of LSSR Onset, 1976–2006, Fixed Effects

starts and zero otherwise. We drop all cases of ongoing spells, given our interest in the initiation of them.

As shown in Figure B.1, the fixed effects results are similar to the findings from the primary analysis. Again, we found that both civil war and population are associated with a stronger likelihood of LSSR onset, while the other control variables fail to reach statistical significance. Again, we find that democracy and democratization are statistically significant, which is line with the results from the primary models. This reinforces the importance of domestic institutions—in particular ones based on electoral elements. In contrast, we again find no significant impact for the other domestic-based variables including both civil resistance variables, INGO presence, and the rule of law. Finally, the international variables again fail to be systematically associated with the probability of LSSR onset. Indeed, while the PTA variable was borderline significant in the main models, it fails to reach significance here. The fixed effects model, therefore, produces results that are basically in line with those from the models in the main text but they raise additional concerns about the efficacy of international factors and prevention of LSSR.

B.1.2 Instrumental Variable Regression

In Figure B.2, we present the results for the instrumental variable regression. Here, we utilize the same model specification from the main LSSR onset models, plus we include rainfall as the instrument for democratization. Based on this analysis, we focus our attention on the impact of democratization on LSSR onset. In line with the discussion above, the democratization variable is negative and statistically significant. This suggests

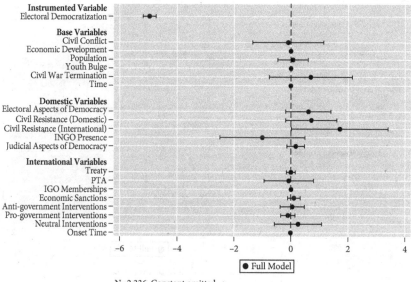

N=2,336. Constant omitted.
Robust standard errors, clustered on country.

Fig. B.2 Determinants of LSSR Onset, 1976–2006, Fixed Effects

that democratic regime change of the government in question is associated with a lower likelihood of LSSR onset, even after accounting for the potential endogenous nature of it.

B.2 LSSR Escalation

B.2.1 Fixed Effects Regression

In this appendix, we use fixed effects regression to check the robustness of the findings from the escalation model. Recall, that to explore this dependent variable we use an ordered response variable. Unfortunately, there is no "off the shelf" fixed effects estimators available when the dependent variable is ordered. To overcome this problem, we estimate two separate models. First, we manually include dummy variables for each spell which acts as a fixed effect for each unit. As discussed earlier, doing this removes the time-constant, cross-sectional heterogeneity that may be the source of omitted variable bias. Second, we employ linear fixed effects regression. While this is not ideal given that the dependent variable is ordered with only three categories (instead of interval-level), it nonetheless provides an additional check on the results while also accounting for the omitted variable problem.[71] We present both models below.

[71] Holding all else constant, the linear fixed effects model is preferable to the nonlinear one because the latter does not drop panels/units with no variation on the dependent variables. Thus, the estimator has some important strengths even if the dependent variable is an imperfect fit for it.

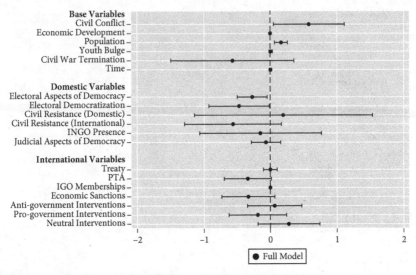

N=2,489. Time and constant variables omitted.
Robust standard errors, clustered on country.

Fig. B.3 Determinants of LSSR Escalation, 1976–2006, Ordered Probit Fixed Effects

Once again, we use the same model specification from above including the same unit of analysis, dependent variable, and independent variables. Overall, both fixed effects models produce results that are largely consistent with the main model and thus we feel more comfortable about the robustness of these findings as well as the conclusions drawn from this work.

Regarding the control variables, the impact of civil conflict is, as expected, positive and statistically significant in both models. This is consistent with the main set of results. In contrast, the youth bulge variable fails to produce statistically significant results in both models even though it was significant in the main regression model. The inconsistent result lends further doubt to the relationship between youth bulges and LSSR.[72] We also fail to see consistent support for the other controls variables (GDP per capita, population, and civil war termination) which is similar to the main models.

Regarding the domestic variables, both models produce consistent results. In line with the main findings, both electoral and judicial democracy are negative as well as statistically significant. This again indicates that democratic institutions appear to be the optimal way to prevent the escalation of large-scale, violent repression. At the same time, we fail to find statistical significance for the other domestic-based variables including democratization, INGO presence, and civil resistance movements. These results are consistent with the main set of models.

Even with alternative specification, we still see weak support for the international variables. In both fixed effects models, economic sanctions are statistically significant and positive. This (again) suggests that this form of international "stick" is associated with a greater probability of escalation. We also see that the other international variables fail

---

[72] As a reminder, we find no relationship between youth bulges in the LSSR onset model.

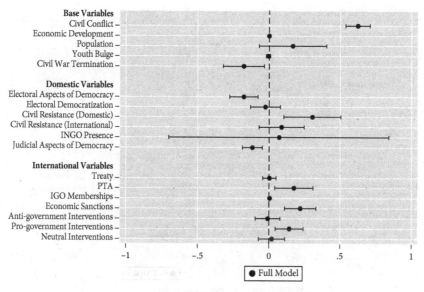

N=2,457. Constant omitted.
Robust standard errors, clustered on country.

Fig. B.4 Determinants of LSSR Escalation, 1976–2006, OLS Fixed Effects

to produce consistent results which is largely consistent with the main set of results. In short, the findings from the fixed effects models are generally similar to the main models, indicating that few factors—mainly electoral and judicial aspects of democracy—can lead to a lower probability of escalation within an LSSR.

We do not present results for the IV regression models given that democratization is not significant in the primary models in the main text.

B.3 LSSR Termination

B.3.1 Fixed Effects Regression

In Figure B.5, we present the results for the fixed effects regression. Like the analysis above, to motivate our investigation we rely on the model specification from the main results. Using spell-year as the unit of analysis, the response variable is LSSR termination which equals 1 the year that the spell terminated, and zero otherwise. Finally, we include the same set of baseline, domestic, and international variables from the earlier estimated models.

Overall, the fixed effects regression produces weaker results compared to the main models. Regarding the baseline variables, civil conflict is negative as expected but, in contrast to the main models, it actually fails to reach statistical significance. We, however, see that the results for the population variable are consistent with the results identified above, as it is linked with a lower probability of LSSR termination. At the same time, the

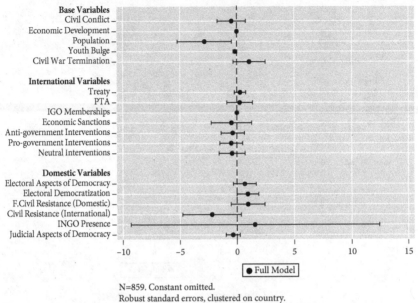

N=859. Constant omitted.
Robust standard errors, clustered on country.

Fig. B.5 Determinants of LSRR Termination, 1976–2006, Fixed Effects

youth bulge and civil war termination variables are in the expected direction but just miss statistical significance. This differs from the main model in which variables reach standard levels of significance. Economic development also fails to produce statistically significant results.

With one important exception, the domestic variables are consistent with the main set of results identified in the analysis conducted in this chapter. As expected, democratization is positive and statistically significant. In contrast to the reported findings, however, the rule of law variable fails to reach standard levels of significance. This suggests that we should interpret the main finding with some caution given the inconsistent results. The level of electoral democracy just fails to reach statistical significance, which is consistent with the findings reported in the chapter. Consistent with identified empirical findings, the other domestic variables are also not significant.

Finally, in line with the primary findings reported in the chapter, the international variables produce weak results. In fact, none of the variables are statistically significant. While this is not unexpected, given our theoretical argument, it is important to note that the IGO membership variable is no longer statistically significant. The inconsistent results suggest that it is again important to be cautious with the potential positive association between IGO memberships and LSSR termination.

B.3.2 Instrumental Variable Regression

As you can see in Figure B.6, the empirical findings suggest that democratization is associated with a greater likelihood of termination, even when accounting for the

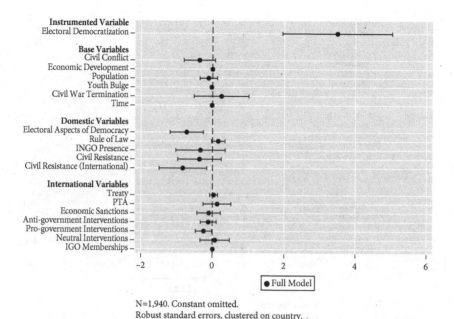

Fig. B.6 Determinants of LSRR Termination, 1976–2006, IV Regression

potential endogeneity issue. While we recognize the challenges that come with esti-
mating IV regression and that we should interpret the results with some caution, they
do compel us to conclude that the primary finding that democratization is associated with a greater likelihood of spell termination is robust to concerns related to
selection effects.

B.4 LSSR Recurrence

B.4.1 Fixed Effects Regression

In Figure B.7, we present the results for the fixed effects model. The sample of governments here includes all countries that previously experienced an LSSR (917 observations
for this sample). The unit of analysis the post-LSSR spell year. We also include a time
measure to account for duration dependence and cluster the standard errors on the post-
spell government.

From our investigation, we see that the results are slightly weaker in the fixed effects
model (especially for the control variables). Indeed, we observe that none of the baseline
variables produce statistically significant results. For example, both GDP and population fail to reach significance even though both were at least borderline significant in
the main model.

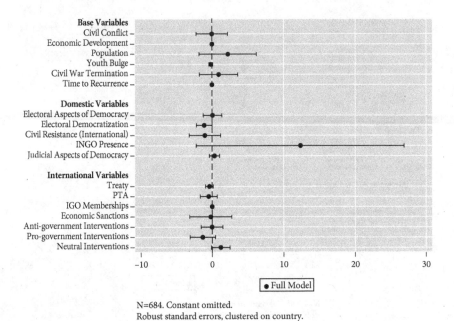

Fig. B.7 Determinants of LSSR Spell Recurrence, 1976–2006, Fixed Effects

More importantly, we see consistent results for the domestic variables, as electoral democratization is still the only domestic-based variable that is statistically significant. Further, we see largely consistent (albeit weak results) for the international variables as neutral interventions are still weakly associated with an higher likelihood of recurrence. The pro-government interventions variable, however, fails to reach standard levels of significance in the fixed effects regression, raising some questions about its impact on LSSR recurrence.

B.4.2 Instrumental Variable Regression

Again consistent with earlier analyses, we estimate an instrumental variable model to ensure that democratization is associated with a lower probability of recurrence after accounting for the potential endogeneity problem. These show general similarities to the main results.

As reported in Figure B, the instrumented electoral democratization variable is negative and statistically significant in the model. The result (which is in line with the primary findings) suggests that newly democratized governments are less likely to engage in LSSRs when compared against nondemocratic governments. The model, therefore, provides further support for the role of electoral democratic institutions in preventing governments from engaging and in this case reinitiating gross human rights abuses.

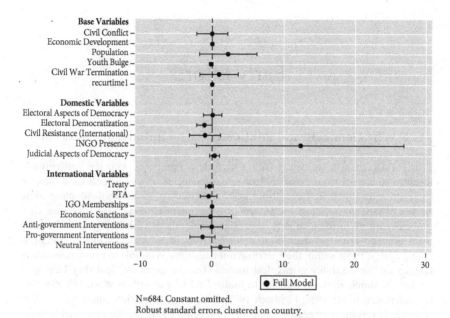

N=684. Constant omitted.
Robust standard errors, clustered on country.

Fig. B.8 Determinants of LSSR Spell Recurrence, 1976–2006, IV Regression

Early Efforts

C.1 Why Genocide and Politicide Ends—Initial Considerations

Nearly a decade ago, we began with a very deep immersion into the conventional literature and tried to understand how to end genocide as well as politicide (despite some attention this topic has still not been addressed systematically). Adopting some version of rationalism, most researchers of government repression (of which we view genocide and politicide a subset) begin their explorations with trying to understand the relevant government's decision to unleash arrests, disappearances, torture, and mass killing against those within their territorial jurisdiction. With this in mind, researchers highlighted the centrality of political leaders (i.e., the executive) and they employed a relatively simple decision calculus to understand why as well as when behavior will be undertaken (Gurr 1986; Lichbach 1987; Davenport 2007; Pierskalla 2010). In this research, government repressive behavior is expected when: (1) the perceived benefits of doing so exceed the costs, (2) there are no viable alternatives for socio-political control and (3) the probability of success from repressive action is low. Although not all components receive the same amount of attention within the rather large amount of research on this topic produced over the last four decades the individual components are worthy of discussion for they framed our initial approach to the topic of interest.

Repressive action is intended to serve as a mechanism to bring about specific benefits to those within government. One of the most important and consistently identified objectives for political authorities concerns staying in office (De Mesquita et al. 2005), but there are others as well: e.g., the establishment/protection of specific political-economic arrangements (Dallin, Breslauer, et al. 1970), the extraction/protection of resources Tilly 1978a, eliminating a particular belief system (Gamson 1975; Goldstein 1978) or establishing quiescence and obedience of those under their rule (Bates 2001; Davenport 2007; Valentino, Huth, and Balch-Lindsay 2004).

Costs are generally thought of in two different ways (Davenport 2007; Krain 2005; DeMeritt 2015). First, the actual use of repression consumes resources in the form of salaries, equipment, human capital, and so forth, which could be used for other purposes. Here, coercion and force is "costly" because authorities have to pay for it—i.e., these are often referred to as "operational costs". Second, costs could emerge in the form of the "backlash" that decision-makers receive from engaging in relevant behavior as those opposing these policies attempt to discourage and/or punish government officials or taking such action (Davenport 2007). In this case, repressive behavior is costly because authorities could lose their jobs for being involved with it or, worse yet, they could lose their lives—these are often referred to as "political costs."

Alternative mechanisms of socio-political control, such as economic cooptation (for material incentives) and political parties (for channeling into existing institutions/practice) influence the repressive decision calculus by providing those in government with options (Dallin, Breslauer, et al. 1970; Lichbach 1987; Krain 1997b). It is largely assumed that if an alternative is available, governments would take it, given the perceived (relative) costliness of coercive and forceful action as well as perceived effectiveness of alternatives.

Finally, the probability of "successful" repressive behavior is considered. For example, governments are generally believed to be utility maximizers and, as such, they would normally attempt to reduce their chances of being unsuccessful at whatever they do. If political authorities have any reason to believe that repression would not go well (e.g., it did not work in the past or their capacity to employ relevant behavior is hindered in some way), then they would be less likely to pursue this course of action (Gurr 1986). If, however, government leaders believed that repressive action was likely to achieve the desired objective, then they would pursue this course of action quickly and wholeheartedly.

With this as the general theoretical orientation to understand the topic, scholars interested in decreasing government repression have consistently advanced a position that this behavior is most likely reduced in its application when the decision-making process and/or the implementation of repressive behavior is disrupted in some way by increasing the costs of relevant action. How is this done, specifically? Well, to understand this, we must first discuss the repressive process.

As conceived, all scholarship on repressive behavior has assumed that there is a political leader or group of leaders who desire staying in power and with this objective in mind they decide when coercive and forceful power should be applied, against whom (the targets of this behavior in terms of identity, size) and with what technique (e.g., political bannings, harassment, beatings, torture, disappearances, and mass killing). The combination reflects the general desire to control (hinder or regulate in some way) and/or eliminate (remove from the ordinary citizenry or from the earth). Collectively, these individuals would be referred to as Principals. It has increasingly been acknowledged that these actors are not the ones who actually engage in the "dirty work" of government repression (Gurr 1986; DeMeritt 2015). Rather, they allocate objectives and tasks to specialists such as generals and police chiefs (i.e., sub-Principals) who, in turn, employ, train, arm, direct, and manage agents who actually dirty their hands beating, arresting, torturing, and killing (i.e., soldiers, police officers, swat teams, prison officials, immigration and border patrol, and militia/death squad members).

Before discussing these strategies however it is important not only to identify what is highlighted by existing research, policy, activism, and advocacy but also to identify what is not. For example, research completely leaves untouched the other parts of the decision calculation (i.e., benefits and perceptions of success) and potentially includes alternative mechanisms of socio-political control albeit without a significant amount of discussion about how precisely this works. Now, there are diverse reasons why this approach has been pursued. For example, it may be the case that researchers believe that neither benefits nor perceptions could be altered and thus there is no reason to discuss these components of the model. It could also be that costs are believed to be far more important for influencing government behavior. Neither of these are discussed explicitly in much detail.

C.1.1 Raising Costs and Stopping Government Violence

In order to increase the cost of engaging in repressive action numerous strategies have been identified. Without question, two have received the largest amount of attention by policymakers, advocates, activists as well as academics. First, it has been argued that external actors could raise the costs of LSSR by imposing economic sanctions on repressive governments in an effort to prompt a positive response—i.e., ending the campaign. Here,

Hypothesis 1—After being threatened by or subject to some form of economic sanction, political authorities are more likely to end ongoing atrocities.

Why would offending government's care about such efforts? Opinions vary. For some, it is maintained that governments care because they do not wish to have their economic situations undermined. In standard realist logic, governments do not wish to have their interests deleteriously influenced and thus they would engage or disengage in whatever activity would protect them the most. For others, governments care about the imposition of economic sanctions because they do not wish to be identified as a violator of norms and seen in a negative light by their peers.

To date, researchers (particularly in the area of international relations) have been skeptical about the possibility of sanction effectiveness—broadly conceived. As Hufbauer, Schott, and Elliot (2008) identify, there are many explanations why sanctions might not have an influence on changing the political behavior of targeted governments. Empirical work has shed little light on this problem because the question has generally not been examined explicitly. With regard to one of the only examinations regarding the influence of economic sanctions on government repression (Wood 2008) results indicate that sanctions increase diverse levels of government coercive and forceful behavior (in this case, the Political Terror Scale). This result was explained by the argument that sanctions threatened the target government and prompted them to exert more effort to retain power. In this context, costs do not seem to be involved and in fact costs appear to give way to benefits. Now, it is clear that this is somewhat different from what we wish to examine here. The measure admittedly encompasses LSSR but it also includes a wide range of lesser activities as well in terms of scope and lethality. The insights provided by this analysis may be useful however.

A second approach to ending repressive spells involves raising the costs of government-sponsored coercive and forceful action by directly interfering with the relevant behavior itself through military intervention. As conceived, in order to curb the aggressive behavior of governments against those under their care, an external actor (a foreign military) is sent into a situation where LSSR is taking place.[73] Differing from the previous solution, in this context government repression is expected to stop not because of a leaders' strategic calculations regarding economic and/or political reputation or survival in general but, instead, because of the government's calculations concerning their ability to carry out their plans/actions in the face of some additional costs. We associate this argument with the following:

Hypothesis 2—When relevant authorities are blocked or physically deterred from engaging in coercive behavior, ongoing atrocities are more likely to end.

The suggestion that intervention is important to repressive behavior was somewhat alien to those involved with researching this topic. As Krain (2005) correctly identified, almost all of the rigorous attention to this policy had been given to the influence of intervention on civil war. Unlike the previous hypothesis, which had been examined once,

---

[73] These situations frequently but do not always involve civil war.

two studies of the intervention-atrocity relationship have been undertaken (Kathman and Wood 2011; Krain 2005).[74]

Within the first of these efforts, Krain (2005) examined atrocities between 1955 and 1997 with ordered logit models for all countries of the world, finding that interventions reduce the magnitude of atrocities when they either directly challenge perpetrators or assist those being victimized. In contrast, interventions that were impartial (i.e., that do not direct their support to one of the combatants) have no impact whatsoever. The lesson from this work is clear as well: when soldiers are put on the ground, they need to be neutral (not favoring either one of the combatants). Without this, the relevant costs of repression would not be perceived by relevant government agents and there would be no impact.

In contrast, although examining the same data and method but extending the investigation up to 2005, Kathman and Wood (2011) found that interventions in general tend to lead to short-term increases in the magnitude of atrocities (especially those that are impartial or pro-target). In further contrast to Krain (2005), these researchers found that pro-target interventions as well as pro-government interventions increased the severity of atrocities over the long term (i.e., 8 years) whereas impartial interventions tended to reduce severity over time. The lesson from this work is clear as well: The lesson from this work is clear as well: when soldiers are put on the ground, they are not likely to change things for the better in the short-term and they are most likely to have a pacifying influence if they are not associated with a particular side.

Viewed through the prism of costs, the differences above seem comprehensible as the different types of interventions involve different types of costs. For example, pro-government military interventions do not impede government spells and, if anything, they might shorten them by reducing costs and facilitating implementation. Pro-challenger interventions could represent a cost but they do not directly impede governments; rather, these represent efforts to side with challengers in their endeavors at competing with governments (generally conceived). Impartial interventions are perhaps the most encompassing and thus the most costly because they are concerned with conflict reduction writ large, as they are not directed toward one particular side but toward dyadic interactions.

Upon reflection, however, the limitations with this work and the necessity for investigating were fairly clear. Although there were two very straightforward policy options that were advanced, the different studies examining them were myopically focused on one policy or the other. No study considered both variables at the same time. Additionally, it was not clear that any of these studies really accepted what most around the world would consider an LSSR. We crafted our investigation into the subject with these insights in mind.

---

[74] DeMeritt (2015) examined the world atrocities database which covers all countries from 1995 to 1999. Within this work, she found that military interventions taken on the side of governments reduced the likelihood that authorities initiated an atrocity whereas military interventions taken on the side of challengers (against governments) reduced the overall severity (i.e., death toll) of the atrocity once underway. The lesson here is clear but different from that identified above: when soldiers are put on the ground, they need to be on one side or the other.

C.1.2 Ending Genocide and Politicide

In an effort to understand what (if anything) stopped LSSR, we focused on what were the most obvious forms of LSSR that received attention (i.e., genocide) as well as a phenomenon that was related (in terms of lethality and scope) but much less popularly discussed because of the controversial nature of its identification and labeling (i.e., politicide). Consistent with the quantitative literature on atrocities and related phenomena, we used the Political Instability Task Force's (PITF) list of genocides and politicides to test our hypotheses on cost-related solutions to ending LSSR (Harff 2003). In these data, there were a total of 41 atrocities from 1955 to 2005 (i.e., genocides/politicides). Our reasoning for using the data was straightforward: Harff (2003, 58) defines genocide and politicide as "the promotion, execution, and/or implied consent of sustained policies by governing elites or their agents . . . that (were) intended to destroy, in whole or part, a communal, political, or politicized ethnic group." This seemed to follow relevant definitions of the phenomenon of interest. In addition to this, a host of high-quality scholarly products had employed these for the evaluation of different hypotheses.

As conceived, the unit of observation in our analysis was the atrocity-month. While many studies that use the PITF data relied on yearly observations to test their arguments, we used monthly-based data for two primary reasons. First and most importantly, this allowed us to more precisely measure our theoretical variables of interest—international military interventions and economic sanctions, providing us with greater confidence about our empirical results. Second, this approach helped minimize problems of endogeneity that have been common in studies involving external interventions. As a robustness check, we re-estimated all of our models using yearly data and our results are consistent with those reported in the main text.

The primary response variable in our analysis was the probability that an atrocity terminates. In our analysis, there were a total of 2,881 atrocity months and 40 atrocity failures; Sudan (beginning in 2004) was the only atrocity that was still ongoing at the time our data ended and it was treated as censored in the statistical models. The average duration of the atrocities in the PITF data was 70 months; Burundi was the shortest one at 2 months and Sudan was the longest atrocity at 230 months.

To code economic sanctions, we used two sources. For the period between 1971 and 2000, we used the monthly data from the Threat and Impositions of Sanctions (TIES) data (Morgan, Bapat, and Kobayashi 2014). Second, for the time period after 2000, we used data from (Hufbauer, Schott, and Elliot 2008). Acknowledging that sanctions could be applied for a wide variety of reasons, we focused on sanctions that were targeted at human rights violations and/or modifying contentious behavior related to conflict and repression undertaken by the actor in question. Based on this, we created a binary variable that equaled 1 when an atrocity experienced economic sanctions, and zero otherwise. As reported in Table 1, sanctions were implemented in 18 atrocities (44 percent). The average number of sanction-months across atrocities with sanctions was 21 months. Sudan experienced the greatest number of sanction-months with 153.

To measure International Military Interventions (IMI), we use the Kisangani and Pickering (2009) update of the Pearson and Baumann data set to operationalize our hypotheses on international military interventions. We focus on the direction of the intervention; specifically, we focused on three intervention types: (1) "pro-perpetrator" where the intervention supported the government and/or opposed rebel or opposition groups when the perpetrator was the government (and vice versa when the perpetrator is a non-government actor), (2) "anti-perpetrator" where the intervention opposed the government and/or supported the rebel or opposition groups when the perpetrator was the government (and again vice versa when the perpetrator is non-government actor), and (3) "impartial" where interventions were coded as non-supportive and/or neutral. Based on these types of interventions, we created three binary variables, one for each intervention type (i.e., pro-perpetrator intervention, anti-perpetrator intervention, and neutral/impartial intervention). We then coded each binary variable a 1 when the atrocity in question experienced the relevant intervention, and zero otherwise. Pro-perpetrator, anti-perpetrator, and neutral interventions are implemented in 16, 20, and 16 atrocities, respectively.

C.1.3 Identifying Control Variables

In line with existing research of the time, we included several control variables that have been commonly associated with the atrocities and related forms of state-sponsored political violence (Davenport 2007; Krain 1997b; Poe and Neal Tate 1994). Specifically, we included three categories of controls: domestic political variables, domestic conflict variables as well as economic and other socio-demographic variables.

Capturing political variables, we created three variables to measure the domestic political context of a government experiencing an atrocity. First, we include a leader durability variable that recorded how many years a leader had been in office. We expect longer tenures to be associated with shorter atrocities. Second, we create a leader failure variable that equals 1 when a leader loses office and zero otherwise. We believe that atrocities would be more likely to end when a leader exited office. Data for both of these variables come from Archigos (Goemans, Gleditsch, and Chiozza 2009). Finally, we create a regime-type variable that equals 1 when the government was a mixed regime, and zero otherwise. Consistent with the extant literature, we consider a government to be a mixed regime if its net Polity score is between −6 and 6 (Marshall and Jaggers 2005).[75] All three domestic political variables are lagged one year.

To address conflict and violence we include three variables to control for the influence of related-conflict processes on the duration of an atrocity. First, we create a variable that equals 1 when the atrocity was also a civil war, and zero otherwise. Second, we create a variable that measured the termination of civil war that equals 1 when the civil war ended and zero otherwise. We expect an ongoing civil war to increase the duration of an atrocity, while the end of one should decrease it. Both variables were from the UCDP/PRIO Armed Conflict Dataset Next, we control for the magnitude of atrocity by including a variable from the Political Instability Task Force data (Goldstone et al. 2005) that equals the cumulative estimates of civilian deaths across the particular year in question. We lag all the conflict variables one year.

We include several variables to account for the socio-economic status of the state in question. Specifically, we include GDP per capita and economic growth. Both variables come from the Expanded Trade and GDP data (Gleditsch 2002). We include a measure of military strength to account for the related concept of government strength. The variable

---

[75] As a robustness check, we include multiple regime-type variables in the analysis (i.e., democracy, nondemocratic, authoritarian, etc.), and all of the results are consistent with the results reported below.

is a ratio of military personnel over total population and is from the Correlates of War data collection (Singer, Bremer, and Stuckey 1972; Singer 1988). Stronger governments— militarily and economically—experience shorter atrocities. Finally, we include a measure of ethnic fractionalization using the ethnolinguistic fractionalization (ELF) index based on data from Mira (1964). We expect more ethnically diverse governments to have longer atrocities. Once again, all of these variables are lagged one year.

C.1.4 Empirical Results

To test our theoretical argument on the duration and termination of atrocities, we employed the well-known Cox Proportional Hazards estimator. To facilitate the effective interpretation and understanding of the statistical findings, the results below are presented as hazard ratios (i.e., exponentiated coefficients). With this metric, hazard ratios above one increase the probability of the hazard occurring (i.e., atrocity fail or termination), while hazard ratios below one decrease the likelihood of atrocity ending. For example, if a hazard ratio is 1.5, then it increases the probability of an atrocity terminating by 50 percent (or 1.5 times) for every one unit change in the variable of interest (i.e., 0 to 1 on economic sanctions variable). Conversely, if it is .75, then it decreases the likelihood that an atrocity will end by 25 percent for every one unit change in the independent variable. We expect both economic sanctions and military intervention variables to be greater than 1, as we hypothesize that both types of external interventions increase the probability that an atrocity will end. As is well known, this model assumes proportional hazards, meaning that the relative hazards of an independent variable is proportional and constant over time. Box-Steffensmeier and Zorn 2001 suggest that when this assumption is violated, it is appropriate to interact the offending variables with some temporal measure. Following their advice, we interact all variables that violate this assumption by the current duration of the atrocity. As a robustness check, we estimated our models using logistic regression and the results are consistent with those reported below.

To further demonstrate the substantive impact of findings, we also present post-estimation survival curves of all the statistically significant variables. The estimated survival functions range from 0 to 1 and are understood as the probability that the event of interest survives past time t having survived up to time t. As a point of comparison, the graphs are akin to predicted probabilities and first differences in that we plot and compare several ideal types. Likewise, we hold all variables at their mean or modal value and alter the covariates of interest.

C.1.5 The Influence of Political and Economic Factors

Overall, the empirical findings show strong support for economic sanctions and impartial interventions. The hazard ratio for the economic sanctions variable is 2.0 and statistically significant (p<.047), indicating that an atrocity is more likely to end when sanctions are enacted. Specifically, an atrocity is 100 percent more likely to terminate when there are ongoing sanctions.

Regarding the substantive impact, at 6 months, an atrocity with economic sanctions is only 0.5 percent more likely to end than one without sanctions, a relatively small substantive effect. However, after 1, 3, and 5 years of economic sanctions, an atrocity is

APPENDIX C: EARLY EFFORTS 179

3 percent, 5 percent, and 10 percent more likely to end, respectively. The results indicate that while the effectiveness of economic sanctions appears to be relatively small at first, it increases over time to a more substantively meaningful impact at 3 years and in particular 5 years. In other words, sanctions can reduce the duration of an atrocity, but it takes time for them to make an impact. This suggests that it is important for the international community to enact sanctions as soon as possible in order for them to have their greatest impact on increasing the probability that they will help bring about the end of an atrocity.

Pro-perpetrator and anti-perpetrator interventions had no substantive effect on atrocity termination (i.e., hazard ratios are basically one) as the variables do not approach statistical significance. Impartial interventions, however, are statistically significant (p<.001); the hazard ratio is 3.6, which suggests that this type of intervention had a strong impact on the termination of an atrocity. In particular, an atrocity was 260 percent more likely to end when there is an impartial intervention, compared to when it lacks an unbiased one. The result is consistent with recent research on this topic that finds impartial interventions reduce the magnitude of atrocities over the long-term (Kathman and Wood 2011).

Finally, we find that impartial interventions have a very strong impact on the duration of atrocities, especially after one year. While an atrocity is 1.1 percent more likely to end when there is an unbiased intervention at 6 months, this increases quickly to 7 percent after one year and 11 percent after three years. By five years, an atrocity is over 25 percent more likely to end when there is an unbiased intervention compared to an atrocity without this type of intervention. The substantive effects indicate that unbiased interventions can dramatically increase the probability that an atrocity ends. At the same time, the results also suggest, similar to the findings for the economic sanctions variable, that it takes some time for the strongest effects to take hold. Thus, it is once again important that the international community act quickly in order to reduce the duration of an atrocity.

C.1.6 Impact for Control Variables

While the statistical and substantive results clearly indicate strong support for our argument, it is also useful to compare our results to the findings for the control variables included in our models. As expected, we find strong support for most of the control variables in line with the expectations of literature focused on government repression/human rights violation. An atrocity was more likely to end when a leader lost office and a civil war ended, while an atrocity was less likely to terminate during an ongoing civil war when the government was ethnically diverse, the atrocity was more severe, and the government was militarily strong. We found no support for regime-type, the time in office for the leader, and the economic variables.

C.2 A Question of Endogeneity in the Study of Genocide and Politicide

The statistical and substantive effects for our key theoretical variables have a strong and consistent statistical and substantive impact on the termination of atrocities. Simply, an atrocity is more likely to end when external actors implement either economic sanctions or impartial interventions compared to when third parties refrain from acting or they pick a side. Despite the strong results, we recognize that some may be concerned that our key variables may be endogenous and our results biased. While we are sympathetic to this argument, we believe that our findings on economic sanctions and neutral interventions are robust to this potential complication.

In statistical terms, the problem is that some omitted variable may be correlated with economic sanctions/military interventions and the error term in our main equation, leading to biased results. To address the endogeneity issue, scholars often employ some type of instrumental variable regression, such as two-stage least squares (2SLS), full information maximum likelihood (FIML), and so forth. While this may work in the theory and in some models, this method is limited in our empirical analyses, due to the important requirement of finding a good instrument (i.e., a variable is correlated with the endogenous independent variable but uncorrelated with the error term in the original equation). Unfortunately, we are unaware of any variable that meets this condition; this is a consequential limitation since weak instruments produce bias and inconsistent results (Bound, Jaeger, and Baker 1995). Thus, due to these limitations, we have decided to avoid instruments and instead show through exploratory and descriptive statistics that our key findings are robust to any biases that may result from endogeneity.

Conceptually, the primary problem is that third parties may select into implementing military interventions or enacting economics sanctions based on the conditions of the atrocity in question. In this way, it is not the intervention that influences the duration of an atrocity, but rather the conditions in an atrocity that make an intervention more likely to occur in the first place. Specifically, the selection effect can take two forms: an external actor may choose to act in relatively difficult atrocities, or conversely, it may select into relatively easy atrocities. While both types of endogeneity are possible, the conventional wisdom in the literature suggests that third parties tend to act in worst-case scenarios (i.e., peacekeepers intervening in difficult civil wars). Fortunately, this type of bias actually favors the null hypothesis, making it more it difficult for find statistical significance for our hypotheses. This is because interventions and sanctions are least likely to be effective when they are implemented in the most difficult situations. However, since we find that sanctions/interventions predict shorter durations despite this bias, we can be confident in the robustness of our results.

Despite the above logic that reinforces our statistical findings, it is also useful to review some basic data on the type of atrocities that third parties intervene in to further alleviate any remaining concerns. To that end, we show that atrocities with and without impartial interventions and economic sanctions share similar characteristics. We focus on death magnitude and duration—two central features of atrocities. In order to conduct this analysis, we measure the average death magnitude and duration up to the first month of the implementation of sanctions and/or neutral interventions. We use the mean duration and death magnitude for the entire length atrocities without sanctions/interventions.

From our investigation, we see that the average (mean) death magnitude across atrocities with economic sanctions is 2.2 compared to 2.4 for atrocities without economic sanctions. The average for impartial interventions is 2.6 and without is 2.3. Thus, the results appear to suggest that there is no selection effect with regard to either type of humanitarianism. Put differently, third parties are not selecting into either relatively difficult or easy atrocities, and our results are free from any biases that result from endogeneity.

The duration of the atrocity is another useful metric. Here, we discuss that the average duration for atrocities with economic sanctions is 81 months compared to 58 without sanctions. The difference of two years is consistent with the argument discussed above that third party select into difficult atrocities. As noted, this type of endogeneity favors the null hypothesis, which makes it more difficult to find statistical evidence in favor our hypothesis. Despite this challenge, we still find that economic sanctions reduce the duration of atrocities, indicating that sanctions are associated with the termination of atrocities.

The average duration for atrocities with impartial interventions is 79 months and for those without impartial interventions is 56 months. Because the average duration is longer for atrocities with impartial interventions than those without it, it is possible that third parties are selecting into relatively easy atrocities. While this is possible, the most likely explanation for this relationship is that external actors are intervening when an atrocity is already nearing an end (i.e., relatively easy). This could be problematic for our results since it could suggest that impartial interventions are not leading to the termination of an atrocity, but rather third parties are only intervening in a neutral way when an atrocity is already ending.

Because this could be a problem for our results, we address this issue empirically by creating a new variable and re-estimating our model. Specifically, we create a new impartial interventions variable that re-codes all interventions that take place within six months of an atrocity ending as zero. The purpose of this robustness check is to ensure that third parties are not choosing to intervene in an atrocity that is already concluding (i.e., easy atrocity). That is, by removing from the analysis all interventions that take place near the end of an atrocity, we can be more confident that the decision to intervene is not related to the termination of the atrocity. In other words, it is unlikely that third parties are selecting into an easy atrocity when the intervention started long before the end of it, as the third party would not have known that the atrocity was coming to an end months prior to its eventual conclusion.

Based on this logic, we replace the impartial interventions variables used in the main analysis with the newly coded one that drops all interventions that took place within six months of the end of the atrocity. As expected, the hazard ratio is greater than one (3.2) and statistically significant ($p<.010$). This indicates that even when we account for the potential concern that third parties are selecting to easy atrocities, impartial interventions are still associated with shorter atrocities. In sum, while we understand that endogeneity is a possible problem with data such as ours, we nonetheless believe that our conceptual discussion and exploratory analysis indicate that our results are robust to any biases that may result from endogeneity.

Bibliography

Acemoglu, Daron, et al. 2008. "Income and Democracy." *American Economic Review* 98 (3): 808–42.

Appel, Benjamin J. 2018. "In the Shadow of the International Criminal Court: Does the ICC Deter Human Rights Violations?" *Journal of Conflict Resolution* 62 (1): 3–28.

Austin, Peter C., and Janet E. Hux. 2002. "A Brief Note on Overlapping Confidence Intervals." *Journal of Vascular Surgery* 36 (1): 194–95.

Ball, Patrick. 1996. *Who Did What to Whom? Planning and Implementing a Large-Scale Human Rights Data Project.* American Association for the Advancement of Science.

Bates, R. H., & Bates, R. H. (2001). *Prosperity and Violence: the Political Economy of Development* (p. 51). New York: WW Norton.

Bellamy, Alex J. 2015. "When States Go Bad: The Termination of State Perpetrated Mass Killing." *Journal of Peace Research* 52 (5): 565–76.

Blanton, Shannon Lindsey. 1999. "Instruments of Security or Tools of Repression? Arms Imports and Human Rights Conditions in Developing Countries." *Journal of Peace Research* 36 (2): 233–44.

Boix, Carles. 2003. *Democracy and Redistribution.* Cambridge: Cambridge University Press.

Bound, John, David A. Jaeger, and Regina M. Baker. 1995. "Problems with Instrumental Variables Estimation When the Correlation between the Instruments and the Endogenous Explanatory Variable is Weak." *Journal of the American Statistical Association* 90 (430): 443–50.

Box-Steffensmeier, Janet M., and Christopher J. W. Zorn. 2001. "Duration Models and Proportional Hazards in Political Science." *American Journal of Political Science* 45 (4): 972–88.

Bratton, Michael, and Nicholas Van de Walle. 1997. *Democratic Experiments in Africa: Regime Transitions in Comparative Perspective.* Cambridge University Press.

Braumoeller, Bear F. 2019. *Only the Dead: The Persistence of War in the Modern Age.* Oxford University Press.

Bueno de Mesquita, Bruce, et al. 2005. "Thinking Inside the Box: A Closer Look at Democracy and Human Rights." *International Studies Quarterly* 49 (3): 439–58.

Butler, Christopher K., Tali Gluch, and Neil J. Mitchell. 2007. "Security Forces and Sexual Violence: A Cross-National Analysis of a Principal—Agent Argument." *Journal of Peace Research* 44 (6): 669–87.

Celestino, Mauricio Rivera, and Kristian Skrede Gleditsch. 2013. "Fresh Carnations or All Thorn, No Rose? Nonviolent Campaigns and Transitions in Autocracies." *Journal of Peace Research* 50 (3): 385–400.

Cheibub, José Antonio, Jennifer Gandhi, and James Raymond Vreeland. 2010. "Democracy and Dictatorship Revisited." *Public Choice* 143 (1–2): 67–101.

Chenoweth, Erica, and Orion A. Lewis. 2013. "Unpacking Nonviolent Campaigns: Intro-ducing the NAVCO 2.0 Dataset." *Journal of Peace Research* 50 (3): 415–23.

Chenoweth, Erica, Evan Perkoski, and Sooyeon Kang. 2017. "State Repression and Nonviolent Resistance." *Journal of Conflict Resolution* 61 (9): 1950–69.

Chenoweth, Erica, and Maria J. Stephan. 2011. *Why Civil Resistance Works: The Strategic Logic of Nonviolent Conflict.* Columbia University Press.

Conrad, Courtenay Ryals, and Will H. Moore. 2010. "What Stops the Torture?" *American Journal of Political Science* 54 (2): 459–76. ISSN: 0092-5853. doi:10.1111/j.1540-5907.2010.00441.x.

Dallin, Alexander, George W. Breslauer, et al. 1970. *Political Terror in Communist Systems.* Stanford University Press.

Davenport, Christian. 1995. "Multi-Dimensional Threat Perception and State Repression: An Inquiry into Why States Apply Negative Sanction." *American Journal of Political Science* 38: 683–713.

Davenport, Christian. 2007. "State Repression and Political Order." *Annual Review of Political Science* 10 (1): 1–23. ISSN: 1094-2939. doi:10.1146/annurev.polisci.10.101405.143216.

Davenport, Christian. 1996. "The Weight of the Past: Exploring Lagged Determinants of Political Repression." *Political Research Quarterly* 49 (2): 377–403. ISSN: 1065-9129. doi:10.1177/106591299604900207.

Davenport, Christian, and David A. Armstrong, Jr. 2004. "Democracy and the Viola-tion of Human Rights: A Statistical Analysis from 1976 to 1996." *American Journal of Political Science* 48 (3): 538–54. ISSN: 0092-5853. doi:10.1111/j.0092-5853.2004.00086.x.

Davenport, Christian, David Armstrong, and Mark Lichbach. 2006. "From Mountains to Movements: Dissent, Repression and Escalation to Civil War." In *International Studies Association Conference, San Diego,* 22–25.

Davenport, Christian, and Molly Inman. 2012. "The State of State Repression Research in the 1990s." *Terrorism and Political Violence* 24 (4): 1–16.

Davenport, Christian, and Cyanne Loyle. 2012. "The States Must Be Crazy: Dissent and the Puzzle of Repressive Persistence." *International Journal of Conflict and Violence (IJCV)* 6 (1): 75–95.

Davenport, C., Rezaee Daryakenari, B., & Wood, R. M. (2022). Tenure through Tyranny? Repression, Dissent, and Leader Removal in Africa and Latin America, 1990–2006. *Journal of Global Security Studies,* 7(1), ogab023.

David Mason, T., et al. 2011. "When Civil Wars Recur: Conditions for Durable Peace After Civil Wars." *International Studies Perspectives* 12 (2): 171–89.

De Mesquita, Bruce Bueno, and George W. Downs. 2006. "Intervention and Democracy." *International Organization* 60 (3): 627–49.

De Mesquita, Bruce Bueno, et al. 2005. *The Logic of Political Survival.* MIT Press.

DeMeritt, Jacqueline H. R. 2015. "Delegating Death: Military Intervention and Govern-ment Killing." *Journal of Conflict Resolution* 59 (3): 428–54.

Downes, Alexander B., and Jonathan Monten. 2013. "Forced to Be Free?: Why Foreign-Imposed Regime Change Rarely Leads to Democratization." *International Security* 37 (4): 90–131.

Escribà-Folch, Abel. 2013. "Repression, Political Threats, and Survival under Autocracy." *International Political Science Review* 34 (5): 543–60.

Fariss, Christopher J. 2014. "Respect for Human Rights Has Improved Over Time: Modeling the Changing Standard of Accountability." *American Political Science Review* 108 (2): 1–22.

Gamson, William A. 1975. *The Strategy of Social Protest* by William A. Gamson. Homewood, Ill. The Dorsey Press, 1975.–iv.

Gassebner, Martin, Michael J. Lamla, and James Raymond Vreeland. 2013. "Extreme Bounds of democracy." *Journal of Conflict Resolution* 57 (2): 171–97.

Gates, Scott, et al. 2010. "Consequences of Conflict in the MENA Region." Background Paper for the World Bank Flagship Report on the Middle East and North Africa.

Gibler, Douglas M., and Kirk A. Randazzo. 2011. "Testing the Effects of Independent Judiciaries on the Likelihood of Democratic Backsliding." *American Journal of Political Science* 55 (3): 696–709.

Gleditsch, Kristian Skrede. 2009. *All International Politics Is Local: The Diffusion of Conflict, Integration, and Democratization.* University of Michigan Press.

Gleditsch, Kristian Skrede. 2002. "Expanded trade and GDP data." *Journal of Conflict Resolution* 46 (5): 712–24.

Gleditsch, Kristian Skrede, and Michael D. Ward. 2006. "Diffusion and the International Context of Democratization." *International Organization:* 911–33.

Goemans, Hein E., Kristian Skrede Gleditsch, and Giacomo Chiozza. 2009. "Archigos. A Data Set on Leaders 1875–2004." *Code Book.*

Goldstein, Robert Justin. 1978. *Political Repression in Modern America from 1870 to the Present.* G. K. Hall & Company.

Goldstone, Jack A., et al. 2005. "A Global Forecasting Model of Political Instability." Annual Meeting of the American Political Science Association.

Greenhill, Brian. 2010. "The Company You Keep: International Socialization and the Diffusion of Human Rights Norms." *International Studies Quarterly* 54 (1): 127–45.

Group, World Bank. 2014. *World Development Indicators 2014.* World Bank Publications.

Gurr, Ted R., and Mark Irving Lichbach. 1986. "Forecasting Internal Conflict: A Competitive Evaluation of Empirical Theories." *Comparative Political Studies* 19 (1): 3–38.

Gurr, Ted Robert. 1986. "The Political Origins of State Violence and Terror: A Theoretical Analysis." *Government Violence and Repression: An Agenda for Research* 45.

Hafner-Burton, Emilie. 2008. "Sticks and Stones: Naming and Shaming the Human Rights Enforcement Problem." *International Organization* 62 (4): 689–716. ISSN: 0020-8183. doi:10.1017/S0020818308080247.

Hafner-Burton, Emilie M. 2005. "Trading Human Rights: How Preferential Trade Agreements Influence Government Repression." *International Organization* 59 (3): 593–629.

Hanmer, Michael J., and Kerem Ozan Kalkan. 2013. "Behind the Curve: Clarifying the Best Approach to Calculating Predicted Probabilities and Marginal Effects from Limited Dependent Variable Models." *American Journal of Political Science* 57 (1): 263–77.

Harff, Barbara. 2003. "No Lessons Learned from the Holocaust: Assessing Risks of Genocide and Political Mass Murder Since 1955." *The American Political Science Review* 97 (1): 57–74. ISSN: 0003-0554. doi:10.1017/S0003055403000522.

Henderson, Errol Anthony. 1998. "The Democratic Peace through the Lens of Culture, 1820–1989." *International Studies Quarterly* 42 (3): 461–84.

Hill, Daniel W., Jr. 2016. "Democracy and the Concept of Personal Integrity Rights." *The Journal of Politics* 78 (3): 822–35.

Hill, Daniel, Jr. 2016. "Democracy and the Concept of Personal Integrity Rights." *The Journal of Politics* 78 (3): 822–35. ISSN: 0022-3816. doi:10.1086/685450.

Hill, Daniel, and Zachary Jones. 2014. "An Empirical Evaluation of Explanations for State Repression." *The American Political Science Review* 108 (3): 661–87. ISSN: 0003-0554. doi:10.1017/S0003055414000306.

Hufbauer, G. C., J. J. Schott, and K. E. Elliot. 2008. *Economic Sanctions Reconsidered.* Washington, DC: Institution for International Economics.

Hughes, Melanie M., et al. 2009. "Power and Relation in the World Polity: The INGO Network Country Score, 1978–1998." *Social Forces* 87 (4): 1711–42.

Kathman, Jacob, and Reed Wood. 2011. "Managing Threat, Cost, and Incentive to Kill the Short-and Long-Term Effects of Intervention in Mass Killings." *The Journal of Conflict Resolution* 55 (5): 735–60. ISSN: 0022-0027. doi:10.1177/0022002711408006.

Keck, Margaret E., and Kathryn Sikkink. 2014. *Activists beyond Borders: Advocacy Networks in International Politics.* Cornell University Press.

Keith, Linda Camp, C. Neal Tate, and Steven Poe. 2009a. "Is the Law a Mere Parchment Barrier to Human Rights Abuse?" *The Journal of Politics* 71 (2): 644–60. ISSN: 0022-3816. doi:10.1017/S0022381609090513.

Keith, Linda Camp, C. Neal Tate, and Steven C. Poe. 2009b. "Is the Law a Mere Parchment Barrier to Human Rights Abuse?" *The Journal of Politics* 71 (2): 644–60.

Kisangani, E. F., and J. Pickering. 2009. "The International Military Intervention Dataset: An Updated Resource for Conflict Scholars." *Journal of Peace Research* 46 (4): 589–99. ISSN: 0022-3433. doi:10.1177/0022343309334634.

Krain, Matthew. 2005. "International Intervention and the Severity of Genocides and Politicides." *International Studies Quarterly* 49 (3): 363–87.

Krain, Matthew. 1997a. "State Sponsored Mass Murder: The Onset and Severity of Genocides and Politicides." *Journal of Conflict Resolution* 41 (3): 331–60.

Krain, Matthew. 1997b. "State-Sponsored Mass Murder: A Study of the Onset and Severity of Genocides and Politicides." *The Journal of Conflict Resolution* 41 (3): 331–360. ISSN: 0022-0027. doi:10.1177/0022002797041003001.

Lichbach, Mark Irving. 1987. "Deterrence or Escalation? The Puzzle of Aggregate Studies of Repression and Dissent." *Journal of Conflict Resolution* 31 (2): 266–97.

Linzer, Drew A., and Jeffrey K. Staton. 2015. "A Global Measure of Judicial Independence, 1948–2012." *Journal of Law and Courts* 3 (2): 223–56.

Lipset, Seymour Martin. 1959. "Some Social Requisites of Democracy: Economic Development and Political Legitimacy." *The American Political Science review* 53 (1): 69–105.

Loyle, Cyanne E., and Benjamin J. Appel. 2017. "Conflict Recurrence and Postconflict Justice: Addressing Motivations and Opportunities for Sustainable Peace." *International Studies Quarterly* 61 (3): 690–703.

Lupu, Yonatan. 2013a. "Best Evidence: The Role of Information in Domestic Judicial Enforcement of International Human Rights Agreements." *International Organization* 67 (3): 469–503.

Lupu, Yonatan. 2013b. "The Informative Power of Treaty Commitment: Using the Spatial Model to Address Selection Effects." *American Journal of Political Science* 57 (4): 912–25.

Mansfield, Edward D., and Helen V. Milner. 2012. *Votes, Vetoes, and the Political Economy of International Trade Agreements.* Princeton University Press.

Marshall, Monty G., and Keith Jaggers. 2005. "Polity iv Project: Political Regime Characteristics and Transitions, 1800–2004 Dataset Users' Manual." *Center for Global Policy, George Mason University, Arlington, VA.*

Mira, Atlas Narodov. 1964. "Moscow: Miklukho-Maklai Ethnological Institute at the Department of Geodesy and Cartography of the State Geological Committee of the Soviet Union."

Møller, Jørgen, and Svend-Erik Skaaning. 2013. "Autocracies, Democracies, and the Violation of Civil Liberties." *Democratization* 20 (1): 82–106.

Morello, C. U. S. 2017. "U.S. Lifts Sanctions on Sudan, Ending Two Decades of Embargo." *The Washington Post.*

Morgan, T. Clifton, Navin Bapat, and Yoshiharu Kobayashi. 2014. "Threat and Imposition of Economic Sanctions 1945–2005: Updating the TIES dataset." *Conflict Management and Peace Science* 31 (5): 541–58.

Nordås, Ragnhild, and Christian Davenport. 2013. "Fight the Youth: Youth Bulges and State Repression." *American Journal of Political Science* 57 (4): 926–40.

Paxton, Pamela, Melanie M. Hughes, and Nicholas E. Reith. 2015. "Extending the INGO Network Country Score, 1950–2008." *Sociological Science* 2:287–307.

Pearson, Frederic S., and Robert A. Baumann. 1993. *International Military Intervention, 1946–1988.* Inter-university Consortium for Political / Social Research Ann Arbor, MI.

Pevehouse, Jon C. 2005. *Democracy from Above: Regional Organizations and Democratization.* Cambridge University Press.

Pevehouse, Jon, Timothy Nordstrom, and Kevin Warnke. 2004. "The Correlates of War 2 International Governmental Organizations Data Version 2.0." *Conflict Management and Peace Science* 21 (2): 101–19.

Pickering, Jeffrey, and Emizet F. Kisangani. 2009. "The International Military Intervention Dataset: An Updated Resource for Conflict Scholars." *Journal of Peace Research* 46 (4): 589–99.

Pickering, Jeffrey, and Mark Peceny. 2006. "Forging Democracy at Gunpoint." *International Studies Quarterly* 50 (3): 539–59.

Pierskalla, Jan Henryk. 2010. "Protest, Deterrence, and Escalation: The Strategic Calculus of Government Repression." *The Journal of Conflict Resolution* 54 (1): 117–45. ISSN: 00220027, 15528766. %5Curl%7Bhttp://www.jstor.org/stable/20684633%7D.

Pinker, Steven. 2011. *The Better Angels of Our Nature. Why Violence Has Declined.* New York, NY: Viking.

Poe, S. C., C. N. Tate, and L. C. Keith. 1999. "Repression of the Human Right to Personal Integrity Revisited." *International Studies Quarterly* 43 (2): 291–313.

Poe, Steven, and C. Neal Tate. 1994. "Repression of Personal Integrity Rights in the 1980's: A Global Analysis." *The American Political Science Review* 88: 853–72. ISSN: 0003-0554. doi:10.2307/2082712.

Power, Samantha. 2013. *"A Problem from Hell": America and the Age of Genocide.* Basic Books.

Przeworski, Adam. 1991. *Democracy and the Market: Political and Economic Reforms in Eastern Europe and Latin America.* Cambridge University Press.

Przeworski, Adam, et al. 2000. *Democracy and Development. Political Institutions and Well-Being in the World, 1950–1990.* Vol. 3. Cambridge: Cambridge University Press. doi:10.1017/CBO9780511804946.

Regan, Patrick M., and Aysegul Aydin. 2006. "Diplomacy and Other Forms of Intervention in Civil Wars." *Journal of Conflict Resolution* 50 (5): 736–56.

Ritter, Emily Hencken. 2014. "Policy Disputes, Political Survival, and the Onset and Severity of State Repression." *Journal of Conflict Resolution* 58 (1): 143–68.

Ritter, Emily Hencken, and Courtenay R. Conrad. 2016. "Preventing and Responding to Dissent: The Observational Challenges of Explaining Strategic Repression." *American Political Science Review* 110 (1): 85–99.

Rummel, Rudolph J. 2002. *Power Kills: Democracy as a Method of Nonviolence.* Brunswick, NJ: Transaction Publishers.

Simmons, Beth A. 2009. *Mobilizing for Human Rights: International Law in Domestic Politics.* Cambridge University Press.

Singer, J. David. 1988. "Reconstructing the Correlates of War Dataset on Material Capabilities of States, 1816–1985." *International Interactions* 14 (2): 115–32.

Singer, J. David, Stuart Bremer, and John Stuckey. 1972. "Capability Distribution, Uncertainty, and Major Power War, 1820–1965." *Peace, War, and Numbers* 19:48.

Spilker, Gabriele, and Tobias Böhmelt. 2013. "The Impact of Preferential Trade Agreements on Governmental Repression Revisited." *The Review of International Organizations* 8 (3): 343–61.

Staiger, Douglas O., and James H. Stock. 1994. *Instrumental variables Regression with Weak Instruments.*

Staw, Barry M. 1981. "The Escalation of Commitment to a Course of Action." *Academy of Management Review* 6 (4): 577–87.

Stephan, Maria J., and Erica Chenoweth. 2008. "Why Civil Resistance Works: The Strategic Logic of Nonviolent Conflict." *International Security* 33 (1): 7–44.

Sullivan, Christopher M., Cyanne E. Loyle, and Christian Davenport. 2012. "The Coercive Weight of the Past: Temporal Dependence and the Conflict-Repression Nexus in the Northern Ireland 'Troubles'." *International Interactions* 38 (4): 426–42. ISSN: 03050629. doi:10.1080/03050629.2012.697005.

Themnér, Lotta, and Peter Wallensteen. 2013. "Armed Conflicts, 1946–2012." *Journal of Peace Research* 50 (4): 509–21.

Tilly, Charles. 1978a. "Collective Violence in European Perspective."

Tilly, Charles. 1978b. *From Mobilization to Revolution.* Reading, MA: Addison-Wesley.

Tyson, Scott A. 2018. "The Agency Problem Underlying Repression." *The Journal of Politics* 80 (4): 1297–1310.

Ulfelder, Jay. 2005. "Contentious Collective Action and the Breakdown of Authoritarian Regimes." *International Political Science Review* 26 (3): 311–34. ISSN: 0192-5121. doi:10.1177/0192512105053786.

Ulfelder, Jay. 2010. "Searching for Sources of Democratic Consolidation." Unpublished. doi:10.2139/ssrn.1703364.

Ulfelder, Jay, and Michael Lustik. 2007. "Modelling Transitions to and from Democracy." *Democratisation* 14 (3): 351–87.

Urdal, Henrik. 2006. "A Clash of Generations? Youth Bulges and Political Violence." *International Studies Quarterly* 50 (3): 607–29.

Valentino, Benjamin, Paul Huth, and Dylan Balch-Lindsay. 2004. "Draining the Sea: Mass Killing and Guerrilla Warfare." *International Organization* 58 (2): 375–407.

Wood, Reed M. 2008. "A Hand upon the Throat of the Nation": Economic Sanctions and State Repression, 1976–2001." *International Studies Quarterly* 52 (3): 489–513.

Wood, Reed M., and Mark Gibney. 2010. "The Political Terror Scale (PTS): A Re-introduction and a Comparison to CIRI." *Human Rights Quarterly* 32: 367.

Wood, Reed M., Jacob D. Kathman, and Stephen E. Gent. 2012. "Armed Intervention and Civilian Victimization in Intrastate Conflicts." *Journal of Peace Research* 49 (5): 647–660.

Young, Joseph K. 2013. "Repression, Dissent, and the Onset of Civil War." *Political Research Quarterly* 66 (3): 516–32.

Zanger, Sabine C. 2000. "A Global Analysis of the Effect of Political Regime Changes on Life Integrity Violations, 1977–93." *Journal of Peace Research* 37 (2): 213–233.

Index

Chile (*continued*)
electoral democracy in 125
extrajudicial killings in 122–123
government terror in 123
human rights violations in 125
"juggernaut" theory and 124
LSSR in 8, 122–125
mass arrests in 122
National Workers Command 123–124
non-violent resistance in 124–125
Operation Condor 123
press, suppression of 123
torture in 122
unions in 123
Vicariate of Solidarity 124
China
LSSR in 8
Soviet Union and 145
Thailand and 145
Vietnam and 145
Chun Doo-Hwan 130–131
civil disobedience. *See* non-violent
resistance
civil society
Chile, in 123–124
democratization, effect on 86, 107
electoral democracy, effect on 19
Madagascar, in 138
Poland, in 134–135
Thailand, in 145
Zambia, in 133
civil war
ongoing civil war
generally 15
across-phase influence of 155
escalation of LSSR, effect on 19,
89–90, 91*f*, 98, 155
independent variable, as 56–57
onset of LSSR, effect on 18, 68–70,
73, 76, 77*f*, 82, 88, 154
recurrence of LSSR, effect on 20,
112, 116, 117*f*, 119
termination of LSSR, effect on
100–101, 101*f*, 106–107, 108*f*, 155
within-phase influence of 155
termination of
escalation of LSSR, effect on 90, 92*f*,
96–97, 153

onset of LSSR, effect on 69, 85*f*
termination of LSSR, effect on 101*f*,
109, 153
within-phase influence of 152
Clinton, Bill 3
cohorts
generally 14, 154–155
Albania, in 127–129
Chile, in 122–125
democratization and 37
"juggernaut" theory, in 14, 33–34
life-cycle approach and 17, 32
Madagascar, in 137–140
Mali, in 141–142
onset of LSSR and 68, 76
Poland, in 135–136
recurrence of LSSR and 111, 113
South Korea, in 131
Sudan, in 7–8
termination of LSSR and 101
Zambia, in 133–134
"commitment escalation of LSSR," 31
Conflict Risk Network (CRN) 3
Congo, Democratic Republic of, LSSR
in 65
Convention Against Torture (CAT) 53
Convention on the Elimination of all
Forms of Discrimination Against
Women (CEDAW) 53
cost-benefit analysis 23
courts. *See* judicial democracy

Darfur Genocide (NGO) 2
Darfur Rehabilitation Project (NGO) 6
Davenport, Christian 56
DeMerritt, Jacqueline H.R. 175n.74
democide 148
democratization
generally 15
civil society, effect of 86, 107
cohorts and 37
electoral democracy (*See* electoral
democracy)
escalation of LSSR, effect on 18–19,
92–93, 94*f*, 153
human rights violations and 27
judicial democracy (*See* judicial
democracy)